SPLAT!

THE MOST EXCITING ARTISTS OF ALL TIME

MARY RICHARDS

SPLAT!

THE MOST EXCITING
ARTISTS OF ALL TIME

Thames & Hudson

CONTENTS

Go to Caravaggio, page 18

Go to Bruegel, page 14

Go to Vermeer, page 26

Go to Velázquez, page 22

Go to Monet, page 42

Go to Rousseau, page 54

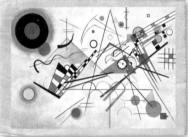
Go to Kandinsky, page 62

Go to Hepworth, page 78

Go to Christo and Jeanne-Claude, page 90

GREAT ARTISTS

Since ancient times, artists have created pictures on the walls of caves, palaces and churches, and made sculptures in buildings and in public spaces. But art is always evolving. New technologies, different materials and fresh ideas change the way people express themselves.

c. 35,000-10,000 BCE

Cave Paintings
All over the world people paint pictures on the walls and ceilings of caves. Paints are made with earth and charcoal mixed with blood, spit or animal fat.

c. 2500-300 BCE

Ancient Egypt
The Egyptians fill their pharaohs' tombs with precious objects for them to enjoy in the afterlife. They paint pictures onto the walls.

c. 1700-200 BCE

Art in China
Artists make objects with finely crafted patterns and designs. An army of clay soldiers is buried with the First Emperor.

c. 1525-1569

Bruegel
paints ordinary people at work and at play in the Flemish countryside. Rich merchants buy his art for their fine homes.

1571-1610

Caravaggio
wows Rome with his dramatic paintings of religious figures. Real people who do not look perfect pose for him in his studio.

1599-1660

Velázquez
lives in the King of Spain's palace. He dazzles the royal family with their portraits. Artists are highly respected for their craft and skill.

1606-1669

Rembrandt
paints incredible self-portraits throughout his life. He observes himself carefully and doesn't hide signs of age.

1632-1675

Vermeer
paints scenes in his Dutch home that are so realistic they look like photographs. Tools such as the "camera obscura" help him to paint accurately.

1840-1926

Monet
develops Impressionism. He paints outdoors instead of staying in a studio. Working quickly, he captures changing patterns of light.

1844-1910

Rousseau
paints in a deliberately childlike style. His wild jungle scenes are filled with exotic animals and plants.

1853-1890

Van Gogh
uses thick brushstrokes and paints quickly to create bold, colourful, expressive art.

1903-1975

Hepworth
makes modern sculptures in stone, wood, bronze and plaster. She is inspired by the landscape of Britain.

1904-1989

Dalí
conjures up fantastical, dreamlike paintings. They combine unusual objects in mysterious, impossible ways.

1907-1954

Kahlo
paints expressive self-portraits that show the way she is feeling. She becomes one of the most recognizable artists of all time.

1912-1956

Pollock
takes his canvas off the easel, and works on the floor. His "action paintings" are enormous, exciting and lively.

CE stands for Common Era. The Common Era began in the first century with year 1. The time before that is known as BCE, which stands for Before the Common Era.

c. stands for circa, which means approximately.

c. 650 BCE – 500 CE

Ancient Greece and Rome
Temples and buildings are decorated with lifelike figures of gods. Artists paint directly onto wet plaster walls to make frescoes.

c. 500 BCE – 1300

The Middle Ages
Wars rage across Europe. As the Christian religion grows, artists are in demand. They begin to set up workshops and take on assistants.

c. 1330–1550

The Renaissance
Artists in Europe decorate churches with Bible scenes. New techniques help them paint accurately. Oil paints are invented.

1475–1564

Michelangelo
makes grand paintings and sculptures on a bigger scale than any other Renaissance artist.

1760–1849

Hokusai
makes prints of life in the Japanese countryside. His art makes its way to Europe on trading ships, where people love his designs.

1774–1840

Friedrich
treks across wild scenery to create pictures that show the power of nature. Landscape paintings become popular across Europe.

1834–1903

Whistler
paints portraits and scenes of London at night. He wants to create a mood and atmosphere in paint.

1859–1891

Seurat
paints grand scenes of Paris using millions of tiny dots. His technique becomes known as "Pointillism."

1866–1944

Kandinsky
makes pictures from shapes, colors and lines that do not look like actual objects.

1881–1973

Picasso
invents Cubism with Braque. They paint violins, guitars and other objects from lots of different angles at the same time.

1887–1968

Duchamp
shocks people by bringing everyday objects into the art gallery. He encourages the question, "What is art?"

1928–1987

Warhol
makes pictures of everyday objects and celebrities in his New York "Factory" studio.

BORN 1929

Kusama
creates rooms that people can enter and explore, often lined with sculptures, mirrors and electric lights.

BORN 1962

Rist
makes films designed to completely surround the viewer as they are projected on the walls, floor and ceiling of the gallery.

ART IN THE BEGINNING

↑ Paintings cover the walls of Tutankhamun's burial chamber. This ancient Egyptian pharaoh ruled around 1336–27 BCE. His tomb was discovered in 1922. The paintings show the story of the young ruler's death and journey to the afterlife. There he meets Osiris, god of the dead.

↑ The Terracotta Army is a masterpiece of early Chinese sculpture, from around 210 BCE. It contains more than 7,000 figures, which lay buried for centuries until being accidentally unearthed by a farmer in the 1970s. Each soldier is lifesize, unique and delicately crafted.

↑ Buffalo and deer run across the walls of the Lascaux caves in France. The caves contain more than 600 spectacular pictures from around 15,000 BCE.

Who made the first work of art, and why? No-one knows for sure. What we do know is that around 35,000 years ago, all over the world, people started painting on the walls of caves. To make paints they mixed colored rocks and earth with animal fat or blood. They worked by firelight, deep in rocky caverns, painting the creatures they hunted, such as bison and deer. Some believe these pictures were part of a magic ceremony designed to bring good luck in hunting. Whatever the reason, since those early times, people have continued to make art. Their pictures tell us about the way they looked at the world and what was important to them.

As the centuries passed, artists became more skilled at making paints and designing tools to carve and model objects. The works they created became more complicated. Around 5,000 years ago, the ancient Egyptians painted detailed pictures on the walls inside their vast tombs. The Egyptians believed that the dead would be able to enjoy them in the next life. In ancient China, the First Emperor was buried in a tomb surrounded by horses, chariots and a whole army of clay soldiers in uniform. They were to guard the emperor and keep him safe. From around 650 BCE, the artists of ancient Greece and Rome started making paintings on the walls of their houses and created grand sculptures in stone to decorate their huge buildings and temples.

We don't always know much about who these early artists were, but as time passed the details of their achievements were recorded. People kept journals and diaries, and from these documents we can piece together the story of great works of art and the lives of the artists who made them.

In the Middle Ages, the Christian religion spread across Europe. Monks illustrated religious books and artists began to paint increasingly realistic pictures on the walls of churches. These pictures were designed to inspire people and help them to remember stories from the Bible. Rich kings and noblemen wanted great works of art for their castles and grand houses, too. Suddenly artists were in demand. Painters and sculptors set up workshops and took on assistants who would learn to work in the style of the "master." If they were talented, these artists would go on to set up their own studios.

Across the world, over thousands of years, artists have created all kinds of art in many different places, from caves and palaces to churches and galleries. The art they have made tells us about the times they lived in and what they believed. It helps bring the past to life.

↑ The great volcano Vesuvius erupted in 79 CE, burying the Roman city of Pompeii. This painting was from a wall in one of the houses. It was preserved under layers of ash and rubble. The well-dressed couple are thought to be a wealthy baker and his wife.

↑ Ancient Greek sculptors wanted to celebrate the perfect form of the human body. This statue is of a great athlete in action. He twists his body round as he prepares to hurl the discus across the field.

↑ In the Renaissance, artists learned to paint lifelike figures who looked like they were standing in real spaces. The Italian painter Giotto decorated this chapel around 1305, filling its walls with art telling stories from the Bible.

MICHELANGELO
A GRAND TASK

THE BIG IDEA	To create grand sculptures and paintings, more lifelike than any artist had ever made before.
CHALLENGES Working on a huge scale; competing for the best jobs with rival artists	**WHO** MICHELANGELO DI LODOVICO BUONARROTI SIMONI **WHAT** Drawings, paintings and sculptures **WHERE** Florence, Rome and other cities in present-day Italy **WHEN** Around 1490 to 1564 **FAMOUS WORKS** *Pietà, Moses* and *David* sculptures; paintings on the ceiling and altar wall of the Sistine Chapel
BACKGROUND	During the time called the "Renaissance," famous artists created large works for grand palaces and churches. Michelangelo was a sculptor in Florence, but went to Rome to paint the Sistine Chapel.

TECHNIQUE
Fresco
A wall painting in which paint is applied to plaster that is still wet.

TECHNIQUE
Perspective
A way of making a flat picture look as if it has depth.

MOVEMENT
Italian Renaissance
- Around 1330 to 1550
- Renaissance means "rebirth." Italian cities were transformed by impressive buildings and churches
- Artists admired Ancient Greece and Rome

NAME: Michelangelo
BORN: 1475
DIED: aged 88
NATIONALITY: Florentine
FAMOUS FOR: being a genius!
As well as a painter and sculptor, Michelangelo was a poet and an architect

→ Michelangelo's Sistine Chapel ceiling tells the story of God creating the world. Can you see God's outstretched hand bringing life to Adam, the first man?

MICHELANGELO
A GRAND TASK

Today, Vatican City is the home of the pope and is the smallest country in the world. In Michelangelo's time, it was part of Rome. Here, you can see the vast church of St. Peter's. The Sistine Chapel is in a building nearby.

Michelangelo came back to the Sistine Chapel in 1536 to paint *The Last Judgement* on the wall behind the altar. The painting shows the day of judgement from the Bible, where human souls are sent to heaven or hell.

Michelangelo copied a nude model to draw this study of Adam for the chapel ceiling. Renaissance artists also practiced drawing the human figure by studying dead bodies.

It's 1508 and Michelangelo is in the Sistine Chapel, the most important Catholic church in the world. Pope Julius II has asked him to create a grand painting to cover its curved ceiling. The artist perches on top of special scaffolding he has designed himself, made of wood and ropes. He works standing up, craning his neck to see the picture he is making. Paint drips on his face. He has sent his team of assistants home and works alone into the night, by candlelight. His feet hurt and his body aches. He is secretive and grumpy, and doesn't want anyone to see the work until he has finished.

Incredibly, although his paintings for the Sistine Chapel are now some of the most famous in the world, Michelangelo hadn't wanted to be a painter. He studied sculpture in Florence, learning by copying the ancient Greek and Roman statues he saw all around him. His sculptures, like the famous *David*, were made from massive blocks of marble that came from a quarry in the nearby mountains of Carrara. People couldn't believe the way Michelangelo managed to make hard, cold stone look like real human flesh. He was a master with a hammer and chisel.

For his frescoes, Michelangelo first made sketches on paper. He then copied them onto the ceiling. A male assistant posed for his study of *The Libyan Sibyl*. You can see how Michelangelo turned the finished picture into a woman.

↑ Michelangelo was a sculptor, not a painter, when Pope Julius II ordered him to paint the chapel ceiling. The pope believed Michelangelo could do anything.

The vast Sistine Chapel ceiling took Michelangelo four years to complete. He used the technique of fresco, which means that the paint is put on while the plaster on the walls is still wet. Michelangelo hadn't done this before, and at first he didn't get the mixture right. The fresco went mouldy and he had to start all over again. Luckily, he had deliberately left the central figures of God and Adam till the end, as he knew his painting would improve. It did!

On the ceiling, Michelangelo painted scenes from the Bible, telling the stories of God creating the world, Adam and Eve, and Noah and the Great Flood. He packed more than 300 lifesize figures into the space. Their dramatic poses show off athletic, muscular bodies. Dressed in billowing robes, they do not look like everyday people. They are perfect, like the heroes of myths and legends. To make the ceiling appear even higher, he painted pictures of towering stone pillars that seem to reach into the sky. It is like looking up into a great temple from ancient times. Nowadays, over five million people visit the chapel every year to marvel at Michelangelo's great work.

Michelangelo said
"Every block of stone has a statue inside it and it is the task of the sculptor to discover it."

ARCHITECT, POET, SCULPTOR

Michelangelo was famous for his sculptures, poetry and architecture as well as for his paintings.

The great dome of St. Peter's church in Rome was designed by Michelangelo, but it wasn't completed until after his death.

Michelangelo wrote hundreds of poems, sometimes scribbled on the pages of his drawings.

David is one of Michelangelo's masterpieces. It stands four meters (almost 14 feet) high, which is more than twice the height of an average man. In the Bible, the young boy David defeated a giant called Goliath, using just one stone.

BRUEGEL
EVERYDAY LIFE

THE BIG IDEA	To make paintings that tell the story of everyday life and ordinary people at work and at play.
CHALLENGES Living in troubled times, when groups were fighting over their different religious beliefs	**WHO** PIETER BRUEGEL THE ELDER **WHAT** Oil paintings, drawings and prints **WHERE** Antwerp and Brussels, in modern-day Belgium **WHEN** 1550s to 1569 **FAMOUS WORKS** Around 40 surviving paintings, including *Children's Games*, *The Hunters in the Snow* and *The Harvesters*
BACKGROUND	In the 16th century, Antwerp was the richest city in Europe. Bruegel painted pictures for its wealthy merchants and bankers. They wanted pictures of the world they lived in to hang on the walls of their houses.

INFLUENCES
- Country festivals and weddings
- The Alps
- The Dutch artist Bosch

TECHNIQUE
Bruegel's drawings were often scratched onto copper plates and turned into prints.

MOVEMENT
Northern Renaissance
- Around 1325 to 1600, in European countries north of Italy
- Artists started using oil paints to make detailed and realistic pictures

NAME: Pieter Bruegel the Elder
BORN: around 1525 to 1530
DIED: aged 44
NATIONALITY: Flemish
FAMOUS FOR: his pictures of the seasons, which are some of the most popular scenes in the history of art

→ Up close, Bruegel's children look more like adults as they play with sticks, hoops, barrels and balls. This is a detail from *Children's Games* (1560). Turn to page 4 to see the complete picture and hundreds of children playing traditional games.

BRUEGEL
EVERYDAY LIFE

↑ *The Painter and the Connoisseur* (1565) might be a self-portrait. It shows an artist working, while a man clutching a pouch of money peers over his shoulder.

↑ In Bruegel's time, busy workshops like this one made hundreds upon hundreds of prints to meet the huge demand for art.

↑ This print is of Bruegel's bizarre drawing *Big Fish Eat Little Fish* (1557). In it, hundreds of tiny fish spill out of the belly and mouth of a large one. There are fish walking on land and flying in the sky, too.

Pieter Bruegel and his friend dress up as peasants and sneak into a country wedding. It is taking place in a barn at the bride's home. Carrying gifts, they pretend to be distant relatives. Nobody notices! They join the merrymakers, sharing bread and pie, pouring ale, and singing and dancing to the tunes the bagpipers play. For these country folk, it's a welcome break from the hard work of daily life – farming the land, harvesting grain and struggling to feed their families.

Bruegel often joined celebrations like this to get ideas for his paintings. His picture *The Peasant Wedding* (c. 1567) is crammed full of lively characters eating, drinking and having fun. Bruegel pays great attention to the expressions on their faces and the details of their clothes.

He trained as a painter in the city of Antwerp. Several hundred artists worked there, and their pictures were popular with wealthy bankers and businessmen. As a young man he traveled to Italy and saw the grand art of Michelangelo and Leonardo da Vinci. But what really inspired him were the breathtaking views of the Alps as he traveled back home.

↑ The bride sits underneath a lantern in the middle of the picture *The Peasant Wedding* (c. 1567). We don't know who the bridegroom is – he might not be there at all. Some people think the bearded man on the far right is Bruegel himself.

↑ *The Hunters in the Snow* (1565). Bruegel's hunters are returning home, with only a single fox to show for their quest. They look out across a frozen lake. A "little ice age" swept across Europe at this time, making the winters bitterly cold.

Bruegel included the stunning scenery he saw in the Alps in *The Hunters in the Snow* (1565). This painting was from a series called *The Months*, which showed peasants at work and play at different times of the year. People are shown hunting, harvesting hay, picking fruit, chopping wood, ice skating, sledding and drinking in a tavern. Until Bruegel, no-one had made such ambitious landscape works – only religious scenes were painted on this scale. These paintings were made for a wealthy merchant from Antwerp, who wanted to hang them on the walls of his grand villa. Five are known to survive today, but there were probably more in the original series. It was once thought that there may have been twelve, one for every month of the year, but now people agree that there were probably six, one for each pair of months. In which case, the view of April and May is still missing!

By the time Bruegel painted these works, he had married and was living in Brussels, another important business center. He was successful there, and was asked by city officials to paint pictures of a new canal being built to connect the city with Antwerp. But Bruegel never started this project – he died at the age of 44. He left two young sons, Pieter and Jan, who both became artists. Pieter was particularly skilled at copying his father's pictures. With his large painting workshop, he made hundreds of versions, which are now in collections all around the world.

EXTRA

CHILDREN'S GAMES

These details from *Children's Games* (1560) show many of the sports and games that we still enjoy today.

People in Bruegel's painting are trying various sorts of gymnastics. Here, the children hang upside down on a wooden bar.

These children are playing with what we would call a "piñata." Using a large stick, they try to open a box filled with treats.

Here, children are playing with whipping-tops. Bruegel also painted children enjoying this popular game on frozen rivers.

CARAVAGGIO
DRAMA IN ROME

THE BIG IDEA	To make dramatic, realistic paintings with a striking use of light and shade.
CHALLENGES Fierce temper; frequently in trouble; had to go on the run at the height of his career	**WHO** MICHELANGELO MERISI DA CARAVAGGIO **WHAT** Oil paintings **WHERE** Rome and Sicily, in present-day Italy; the island of Malta **WHEN** 1592 to 1610 **FAMOUS WORKS** *Boy with a Basket of Fruit*, *The Calling of St. Matthew*, *The Beheading of John the Baptist*
BACKGROUND	The Catholic Church wanted ordinary people to understand the stories of the lives of Christ and the saints. Caravaggio's pictures showed Jesus and the saints as real people, in real settings.

TECHNIQUE
Caravaggio set up his models in a dark room. Light shone onto them from a lamp or high window.

INFLUENCES
• Grand works of the Italian and Northern Renaissance
• Criminal life in the streets of Rome

MOVEMENT
BAROQUE
• Around 1600 to 1700
• Artists make bold, theatrical paintings
• Pictures become even more detailed and realistic
• Striking use of light and shadow

NAME: Caravaggio
BORN: 1571
DIED: aged 38
NATIONALITY: Italian
FAMOUS FOR: using models he'd found on the streets of Rome; painting gory details; killing a man

→ *The Calling of St. Matthew* (1600) looks as if it might be set in a gambling den in Caravaggio's Rome. It tells the Bible story of Matthew, a tax collector, being called to follow Jesus. Light pours in from the window, suggesting the presence of God.

CARAVAGGIO
DRAMA IN ROME

Caravaggio tears through the city streets. He's in trouble again ...

Caravaggio's model for *Boy with a Basket of Fruit* (1593) may have been fellow artist Mario Minniti. Caravaggio painted it shortly after arriving in Rome.

In the *Madonna of the Pilgrims* (1604–06), Caravaggio paints the Virgin Mary with bare feet and rough, dirty toenails.

Caravaggio painted his own face onto the bleeding, severed head of the defeated giant Goliath in *David with the Head of Goliath* (c. 1610).

Michelangelo Merisi da Caravaggio runs through the seedy backstreets of Rome. It's 1601, late at night, and he's been in a fight in a tavern – again. Caravaggio looks wild and frightening, with dark, messy hair and thick eyebrows. He carries a dagger beneath his cloak. Although he is becoming a famous artist and lives in the palace of a Roman cardinal, Caravaggio eats and drinks with his old friends in narrow, dirty streets, where violent criminals lurk in the shadows. It seems a strange place for a painter whose religious scenes decorate the finest churches in the city.

Yet it was on the streets of Rome that Caravaggio found the men and women he used to pose for his pictures. And he painted them exactly as he saw them, with sunburned skin, dirty fingernails and torn clothing. Some people were outraged, and asked him to paint differently so as not to upset anyone. Who wanted to see beggars and criminals in dingy settings posing as Jesus, the Virgin Mary or the saints? But others in the Catholic Church believed that Caravaggio's fresh take on Bible stories was just what was needed to keep ordinary people interested in going to church.

In *The Cardsharps* (c. 1594), two boys play cards, but the one on the right is cheating. He hides extra cards behind his back. His accomplice has holes in the fingers of his gloves that help him in his card tricks.

↑ Jesus stretches out his hand to bless the food on the table. He seems to be inviting us into *The Supper at Emmaus* (1601).

↑ For centuries before the invention of the paint tube, artists like Caravaggio stored their paints in pig bladders. They squeezed out the amount of paint they needed as they worked.

Caravaggio was born in Milan, but moved to Rome in 1592 to become an artist. He was soon noticed by the wealthy Cardinal Francesco del Monte, who let him stay in his palace in exchange for works of art. He also helped Caravaggio to get his biggest job yet, painting for the Contarelli Chapel in the Church of San Luigi dei Francesi in Rome. Caravaggio refused to paint directly onto the walls like other artists. Instead, he worked with oil paints on huge canvases in his studio, which were hung in the church afterward. He painted these works – including *The Calling of St. Matthew* – using real models, props and dramatic lighting. He set up the scene in a darkened space, and shone a bright light onto the figures. It must have looked rather like he was setting up a scene for a film, as a director would today.

Caravaggio's work took Rome by storm, and his pictures were in demand. But his behavior got worse and worse. Police documents from the time record the violence of Caravaggio and his friends. In 1606 he killed a man in a fight, probably over a gambling debt. This crime was punishable by death. Fearing for his life, Caravaggio went on the run. He traveled south, to Naples, Malta, then Sicily. Along the way, he painted stunning works like *The Beheading of John the Baptist* (1608), but he also got into more trouble with the law. He tried to make his way back to Rome, where he believed he might be pardoned. But in 1610, weak and alone, he collapsed while suffering from a high fever and died.

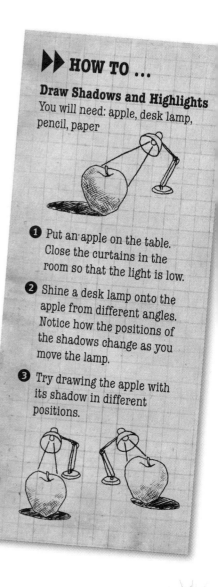

▶▶ **HOW TO ...**

Draw Shadows and Highlights
You will need: apple, desk lamp, pencil, paper

1 Put an apple on the table. Close the curtains in the room so that the light is low.

2 Shine a desk lamp onto the apple from different angles. Notice how the positions of the shadows change as you move the lamp.

3 Try drawing the apple with its shadow in different positions.

VELÁZQUEZ
FIT FOR A KING

## THE BIG IDEA	To paint realistic portraits that capture the likeness and personality of their subjects.
## CHALLENGES A slow worker; royal duties for the king took up lots of his painting time	**WHO** DIEGO RODRÍGUEZ DE SILVA Y VELÁZQUEZ **WHAT** Oil paintings **WHERE** Madrid, in Spain **WHEN** 1611 to 1660 **FAMOUS WORKS** *Las Meninas*, *The Waterseller of Seville*, *Old Woman Cooking Eggs*, *Innocent X*, portraits of Philip IV of Spain
## BACKGROUND	Philip IV, King of Spain, was young, ambitious and passionate about art. He chose Velázquez to make paintings that celebrated his achievements and his beautiful family.

TECHNIQUE
Velázquez painted "alla prima," which means onto wet background paint. This made his brushstrokes look soft and feathery.

INFLUENCES
His dramatic use of light and shade was influenced by Caravaggio and Titian.

NAME: Diego Velázquez
BORN: 1599
DIED: aged 61
NATIONALITY: Spanish
FAMOUS FOR: dazzling likenesses of his subjects; becoming a nobleman; undertaking royal duties

→ The king sent Velázquez's portraits of his daughter to her future husband, Emperor Leopold I of Austria. The idea was to show him how beautiful she was. In this picture, *Infanta Margarita Teresa in a Blue Dress* (1659), she is only eight years old!

VELÁZQUEZ
FIT FOR A KING

Velázquez is the only artist allowed to paint the portrait of the king ...

↑ One of Velázquez's favorite portraits of the king was *Philip IV of Spain in Brown and Silver* (c. 1631–2). We know this because he decided to sign it on the letter Philip is holding.

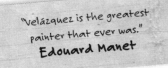

"Velázquez is the greatest painter that ever was."
Edouard Manet

↑ Velázquez painted this *Portrait of Innocent X* (1650) on a visit to Rome. When the pope saw it, he gasped, "Too real!" Extremely impressed by Velázquez, he wrote to the king, supporting the painter's knighthood.

Diego Velázquez looks up. It's 1623, and he's just finished a picture of the Spanish king, Philip IV. The likeness is incredible. He's captured Philip's long face, piercing eyes and thoughtful expression. The king is amazed. He's so impressed he decides that he won't let anyone else paint him ever again.

Velázquez was an exceptional child. At only ten years old he began training as an artist in the Spanish city of Seville. By 18 he had set up his own workshop. Early on, he painted pictures of ordinary people in taverns and kitchens. *Old Woman Cooking Eggs* (1618) is one of these. The eggs look so real you can almost smell them frying in the pan.

Velázquez's talents were soon put to the test. At the young age of 24, he was appointed court painter to Philip IV (who was actually only a year older than him). This job led to a rapid rise in fame, and made Velázquez one of the most important members of the royal household.

↑ Velázquez painted *Old Woman Cooking Eggs* (1618) when he was just 19 years old. He contrasts the hollow cheeks and weathered hands of the old woman with the smooth, plump face of the boy.

↑ Velázquez painted himself into *Las Meninas* (1656, detail), a dazzling portrait of five-year-old Princess Margarita and her maids. He's on the left, holding his paintbrush. The king and queen are reflected in the mirror on the wall.

Velázquez moved to Madrid to live in the royal palace. At the time, artists were not thought of very highly, and he was paid no more than the royal hairdresser! However, Velázquez rose through the ranks, taking on more and more important jobs. As well as painting, he organized royal gatherings and parties. The king also sent him to Italy to buy more paintings to decorate the palace.

Velázquez's striking pictures of the king, his daughter the Infanta Margarita and the rest of the royal family are considered some of the greatest portraits ever made. Their magnificent costumes gave Velázquez the chance to show his incredible skill at painting different textures, such as lace, precious jewels and shining armor. He also painted pictures of the jesters and dwarves who lived in the palace for the entertainment of the royal family. The king even took Velázquez to paint him out hunting and in battle. In 1644, at war with France, he posed for Velázquez in a studio set up in the Spanish army headquarters.

Just before Velázquez died, the king made him a Knight of the Order of Santiago, which was the highest honor in the land and unheard of for a painter. Velázquez was so proud of his knighthood that he went back to his masterpiece, *Las Meninas*, to paint the Order's red cross on his chest.

VERMEER
LIFE AT HOME

THE BIG IDEA	To paint simple scenes of life at home, so realistic that they almost leap off the canvas.
CHALLENGES Money worries; a large family to support; used expensive paints; worked slowly	**WHO** JOHANNES VERMEER **WHAT** Oil paintings **WHERE** The city of Delft, in the Netherlands **WHEN** 1653 to 1675 **FAMOUS WORKS** 36 paintings survive, including *The Milkmaid*, *The Art of Painting*, *Girl with a Pearl Earring* and *The Music Lesson*
BACKGROUND	Vermeer lived in the "Golden Age" of Dutch art. Scenes of everyday life, known as "genre" paintings, were very popular. Vermeer painted people at home, cooking, sewing and making music.

TECHNIQUE
Vermeer made paints using natural pigments, or colors. They were mixed with oil and then ground to make a smooth paste.

INFLUENCES
- The craftsmanship of fine musical instruments
- Other Delft artists, such as Fabritius and de Hooch

NAME: Johannes Vermeer
BORN: 1632
DIED: aged 43
NATIONALITY: Dutch
FAMOUS FOR: paintings that look like photographs; mysterious techniques; setting all his pictures in the same room

→ The young woman in Vermeer's most famous painting, *Girl with a Pearl Earring* (c. 1665), looks straight at us. Her bright turban is painted in Vermeer's favorite color, ultramarine blue. This paint was as precious as the pearls she was wearing.

VERMEER
LIFE AT HOME

↑ In *The Art of Painting* (1666–68) Vermeer paints an artist at work in a studio very like the one he worked in. On the left hangs a thick tapestry, drawn back like a curtain. It's as if we are looking through a real window at the scene inside the room.

↑ Vermeer loved to include musical instruments in his paintings. The guitar in this picture, *The Guitar Player* (c. 1672), was probably borrowed from a wealthy collector.

↑ Vermeer's picture *The Milkmaid* (c. 1658) is so realistic it looks like a photograph. The simple action of a servant pouring milk from a jug seems to be frozen in time.

Johannes Vermeer is working in the studio he has set up in two rooms on the second floor of his home on Delft's market square. He lives there with his wife, Catharina, their young children and his mother-in-law, Maria Thins. It's 1658. A young woman, dressed in the white hat and thick skirts of a kitchen maid, poses for a picture. She stands at a table preparing food, pouring milk from a jug into a bowl. Vermeer thinks about how he will capture this in paint. The flowing white liquid catches the light from the window, and he adds highlights with a few fine strokes of his brush. Vermeer steps back to take a look at his picture. He has transferred the scene in front of him onto the canvas perfectly, as if by magic. The colors seem to glow even more brightly than in real life. How has he done this?

↑ Children play under a bench in *The Little Street* (1657–58, detail). This is the only picture in which Vermeer included children, even though he had 15 of his own.

Vermeer's methods are cloaked in secrecy – he didn't have any pupils, and left no record of the way he worked. Many people now believe that Vermeer and other artists of his time used special tools with mirrors and lenses to project images onto canvas. These would have helped them to copy precisely what they saw in the room. The use of lenses might also explain the blurry or 'out-of-focus' way that Vermeer paints shiny objects like pearls and gold picture frames. But there is no written evidence. The only clues are in his paintings.

Vermeer lived in the Dutch city of Delft. Although he sold some of his paintings in his lifetime, Vermeer only became world famous several centuries after he died. He spent much of his time working as an art dealer, to earn money to support his 15 children. People in Delft liked buying art, but times could be tough. When Vermeer died at the age of 43, his wife described how he had 'fallen into a frenzy', hugely in debt and worried about how he could support his large family.

Only 36 paintings by Vermeer are known to survive, making them extremely rare and valuable. People are intrigued by Vermeer's techniques and by his mysterious subjects. Who were the young women posing for him, and what were their lives like? We will never know the answers to these questions, but Vermeer makes us wonder …

EXTRA

TRICKS OF THE TRADE

New inventions, materials and techniques helped Vermeer to create ever more realistic pictures.

The camera obscura helped artists make their pictures. The artist sat in a dark cubicle. Light passed through a hole in the wall, fitted with a lens, projecting an image of the scene onto canvas.

Vermeer used rich colours, especially ultramarine blue made from a precious stone called lapis lazuli. It was expensive and came from Afghanistan.

Experts use x-rays and infra-red cameras to see how Vermeer made his pictures. They show that he often changed his mind while working, painting over figures, objects or details along the way.

HOKUSAI
MAKING WAVES

THE BIG IDEA	To create prints of the natural world and everyday scenes of Japanese life.
CHALLENGES Often poor; designs were controlled and had to carry an official seal of approval	**WHO** **KATSUSHIKA HOKUSAI** (but he used many different names) **WHAT** Drawings, paintings and woodblock prints **WHERE** Edo (present-day Tokyo), in Japan **WHEN** 1790s to 1849 **FAMOUS WORKS** *The Great Wave off Kanagawa* and other scenes from the print series *Thirty-Six Views of Mount Fuji*
BACKGROUND	By 1800 there were hundreds of woodblock print publishers in Edo (Tokyo). Hokusai didn't want to make the same pictures as everyone else. His pictures of nature and everyday life challenged tradition.

TECHNIQUES
To make a woodblock print, an image was carved into a block by a block carver. Ink was applied and it was printed onto paper.

INFLUENCES
- Birds, plants and wildlife
- Chinese art of the Ming Dynasty
- The Japanese 15th-century painter Sesshu

NAME: Hokusai
BORN: 1760
DIED: aged 90
NATIONALITY: Japanese
FAMOUS FOR: pictures of Japan's Mount Fuji; scenes of the countryside around Edo; working under different names

→ Hokusai's art celebrated the stunning scenery of Edo and its surroundings. For *The Amida Falls*, from the series *A Tour of Waterfalls in Various Provinces* (c. 1827-35), he used intense Prussian blue ink, which had just become available in Japan. It was made from chemicals rather than natural dyes.

HOKUSAI
MAKING WAVES

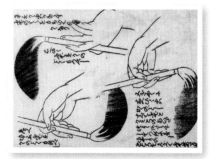

↑ Hokusai produced manuals for students with step-by-step instructions showing how to draw figures, animals and other objects. They contained thousands of sketches of characters in different costumes and poses.

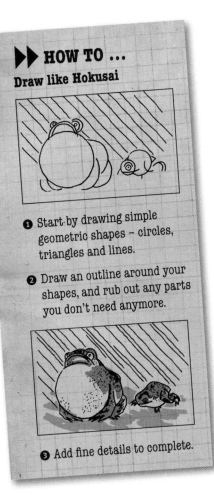

▶▶ HOW TO ...
Draw like Hokusai

❶ Start by drawing simple geometric shapes – circles, triangles and lines.

❷ Draw an outline around your shapes, and rub out any parts you don't need anymore.

❸ Add fine details to complete.

It's a spring day in 1806. Katsushika Hokusai has been called to the palace of the shogun, Japan's military leader, to make a giant painting as part of a competition with another artist, Buncho. Hokusai dips one of his huge brushes into a vast pot of India ink, and draws a twisting river. Then, to everyone's surprise, he takes a chicken, dips its feet in paint and lets it walk across the giant roll of paper. Its footprints leave marks that look like fallen maple leaves. Buncho admits defeat – everyone is amazed at Hokusai's inventiveness!

Hokusai was born in Edo (modern-day Tokyo). As a teenager he worked in a woodblock-cutting workshop, then joined the studio of Shunsho, an artist famous for producing woodblock prints of actors from Edo's Kabuki theater. The pictures were of characters dressed in colorful, elaborate costumes, and were very popular with Edo's wealthy merchants. They bought them as souvenirs of the magnificent shows they had seen. But before long, Hokusai was keen to take on new challenges. He started experimenting with different subjects, such as landscapes and nature studies, and was thrown out for not following tradition.

↑ In this view of a lumber yard, Hokusai used the Western technique of perspective. This means the scene has depth and space, rather than being flat. *Tatekawa in Honjo* is from the series *Thirty-Six Views of Mount Fuji* (c. 1826–33).

↑ Snow-capped Mount Fuji is just visible in the background, dwarfed by a giant wave, which seems to be swallowing three boats like a sea monster. *The Great Wave off Kanagawa* is from the series *Thirty-Six Views of Mount Fuji* (c. 1826–33).

Hokusai was often poor, because he didn't always produce the kind of works people wanted to buy. His most successful works, albums of views of Edo, were not published until he was in his seventies. He wrote, "nothing I did before the age of 70 was worthy of attention." *Thirty-Six Views of Mount Fuji* (1826–33) gives a snapshot of life in the villages and countryside around Edo – peasants, fishermen, travelers and views of landscapes. The famous volcano is in the background of every scene. Hokusai's bold lines, vivid colors and dramatic shapes inspired other artists to work on landscape views. They also had a huge influence on European artists, such as the Impressionists in Paris.

Hokusai seemed to love change. He used around 30 different names throughout his long career. For instance, as he got older he signed many of his prints "Old Man Mad About Drawing," and he moved house 90 times! In all, he made around 30,000 designs – 250 books and 3,500 prints as well as drawings, paintings and even a set of prints that people could cut out, making their own 3D scenes, called "dioramas."

↑ The snow-capped Mount Fuji, Japan's highest mountain, soars high over rice fields. Hokusai included it in many of his pictures, including *The Great Wave off Kanagawa* (above). It's actually a volcano, but it hasn't erupted since 1707.

FRIEDRICH
WILD NATURE

THE BIG IDEA	To paint dramatic landscapes that show the awesome power of nature – wild, vast and breathtakingly beautiful.
CHALLENGES Regular bouts of unhappiness; it was almost impossible to paint after he had a stroke	**WHO** CASPAR DAVID FRIEDRICH **WHAT** Oil paintings, drawings in pencil and ink **WHERE** Dresden, in Germany **WHEN** 1794 to 1835 **FAMOUS WORKS** *The Cross in the Mountains*, *The Monk by the Sea*, *Wanderer Above the Sea of Fog* and *The Sea of Ice*
BACKGROUND	In the 18th and 19th centuries, artists, writers and musicians across Europe were part of the "Romantic" movement. Friedrich's moody landscape pictures communicated his feelings about life and death.

TECHNIQUES
Friedrich made detailed drawings with pencil and sepia ink – a brown paint made from the ink of a cuttlefish.

INFLUENCES
- Walking in forests and mountains
- The rugged Baltic coastline
- Crumbling ruins

MOVEMENT
ROMANTICISM
- Around 1780s to 1850s
- Artists, musicians and poets rebelled against the strict rules of classical painting, music and literature
- Works show the power of nature or the horrors of war

NAME: Caspar David Friedrich
BORN: 1774
DIED: aged 65
NATIONALITY: German
FAMOUS FOR: pictures of wild nature; going on sketching trips to remote places; teaching at the Dresden Academy

→ The man in *Wanderer Above the Sea of Fog* (1818) stares out from the mountaintop. Is he looking down from on high like a God having conquered nature? Or is he trying to tell us that nature is more powerful than mankind?

FRIEDRICH
WILD NATURE

It's 1801 and strong winds blow in from the Baltic Sea on the island of Rügen. Caspar Friedrich treks across the chalk cliffs with his sketchbooks on his back. He's come to draw the scenery, but he'll take his pictures back to finish in the studio.

Friedrich grew up in a small town on the Baltic coast. He was one of ten children, and had a tough childhood. His mother died when he was just seven, and when he was only 13 years old he watched one of his brothers drown while skating on a frozen pond. He also lost two sisters. Many believe that these tragedies shaped the way he thought about life.

After studying art in Copenhagen, Friedrich moved to Dresden. Here he made expeditions to nearby mountains and forests, where he would sketch and draw rocky peaks and woodlands thick with fir trees. At the age of 33, he took up oil painting. One of his first oil paintings was a picture made for the altar of a church – *The Cross in the Mountains*. It shocked its viewers. At the time, it was very unusual for landscapes to be used as the subject of religious pictures, and here the trees, sunset and mountain peak seem to overpower the tiny figure of Christ on the cross.

↑ Friedrich said the evergreen fir trees, rocky mountain and sun's rays in *The Cross in the Mountains* (1808) stood for faith and hope. He designed the gold frame himself, and it was carved by an artist friend.

Friedrich said
"I have to stay alone in order to fully contemplate and feel nature."

↑ In 1818, Friedrich and his wife, Caroline, toured Rügen and the Baltic coast. Around that time, he made paintings of figures in landscapes such as *The Chalk Cliffs on Rügen* (1818).

↑ In this moody, night-time scene, a group of monks carry a coffin to a grave in a snow-covered churchyard. A ruined abbey towers over the tiny figures. *Abbey in the Oakwood* (1809-10) was one of the first oil paintings Friedrich exhibited.

↑ A tiny ship is dwarfed by great shards of ice. *The Sea of Ice* (1823-24) was inspired by the story of an Arctic expedition that ended in disaster. *HMS Fury* was wrecked on the ice and had to be abandoned.

Success came to Friedrich a few years later when his paintings *The Monk by the Sea* and *Abbey in the Oakwood* were shown at an exhibition in Berlin and bought by the young Frederick William, Crown Prince of Prussia. Other future collectors would include Tsar Nicholas I of Russia and the Russian poet Zhukovsky, who became Friedrich's friend and helped him to sell his work. He liked the way Friedrich seemed to pour his feelings and imagination into his pictures. Jagged rocks, crumbling ruins and dark, stormy skies showed a world that was too powerful to tame. These scenes often included tiny figures dwarfed by rugged landscapes. Friedrich was a religious man, and was also inspired by ancient tales of Norse gods from myths and legends. He preferred painting sunrise, sunset or moonlight views, and didn't usually paint daylight scenes. He often suffered from bouts of unhappiness, and at these times vultures, owls, graveyards and ruins were often included in his work.

Friedrich continued living in Dresden, eventually becoming a professor at its art academy, where he had taught for many years. Sadly, in the last years of his life, a stroke left him paralyzed, and he was hardly able to paint. He got by with the help of artist friends and collectors. But his powerful art, which had a great impact on everyone around him, lived on.

EXTRA

THE ROMANTICS

Romantic artists, poets and musicians expressed their strong feelings and passions in their work.

The Romantics loved the idea of otherworldly powers. In Mary Shelley's book *Frankenstein*, a scientist brings to life a hideous and terrifying monster.

Medieval folk tales and legends inspired great works of Romantic art. Wagner's dramatic operas set these traditional stories to music.

The Romantics were obsessed with the power of nature. J.M.W. Turner tied himself to the mast of a ship to paint *Snow Storm - Steam-Boat off a Harbor's Mouth* (1842).

WHISTLER
ART AND MUSIC

THE BIG IDEA	To paint landscapes and portraits that create a mood, without needing to tell a story.
CHALLENGES His art is criticized; goes bankrupt after an expensive court case to defend his work	**WHO** JAMES ABBOTT McNEILL WHISTLER **WHAT** Oil paintings, etchings and interior design **WHERE** Paris, in France and London, in England **WHEN** 1855 to 1903 **FAMOUS WORKS** *Arrangement in Grey and Black No. 1* (a painting of his mother); night scenes called *Nocturnes*; the Peacock Room
BACKGROUND	Whistler moved from America to Europe in 1855. The art academies in London and Paris liked to show grand, polished paintings of scenes from history. Whistler wanted to do something different.

TECHNIQUES
Whistler mixed his oil paints with copal resin, linseed oil and turpentine, a special recipe that he called his "sauce."

INFLUENCES
• Fine food, dressing elegantly and throwing parties
• The portraits of Velázquez
• The River Thames

MOVEMENT
THE AESTHETIC MOVEMENT
• 1870s to 1880s in London
• Artists, designers and architects believed that art was more important than anything else
• Inspired by Asian art and design

NAME: James Whistler
BORN: 1834
DIED: aged 69
NATIONALITY: American
FAMOUS FOR: defending his art in court; decorating a room in the Japanese style; moody night scenes

→ Look at the way Whistler uses paint in *Nocturne in Black and Gold – The Falling Rocket* (1875). Sparks and clouds of smoke light up the night sky. His picture captures the atmosphere of a firework display he saw by the River Thames in London.

WHISTLER
ART AND MUSIC

↑ *Nocturne in Blue and Silver – Chelsea* (1871) is one of Whistler's many moody scenes of the River Thames. "Nocturne" is a French word meaning "night." For him, night was a magical time when the river was "cloaked in mist, like a veil" and its warehouses became "palaces."

↑ In the 1860s, Whistler stopped signing his pictures and letters with his name. Instead, he used a "butterfly" signature he invented, inspired by Chinese and Japanese designs.

↑ This photograph of Whistler's mother shows us that his painting (opposite) was a very accurate portrayal, even though he said that wasn't his plan.

It's autumn 1871. James Whistler has been on a boat trip on the River Thames with his mother. For days he's been painting her portrait, and decides he needs some fresh air. They arrive home in Chelsea just before sunset. Whistler looks out at the view of the river from his front gate – it's dark, misty and calm. He's so moved by its beauty that he rushes upstairs to paint the scene before the light fades. Afterward, he asks his neighbor, who owns a boat, to take him out again at night so he can make more of these pictures.

Whistler, who grew up in America, studied art in Paris before moving to London. Here, he became friends with artists and writers such as Dante Gabriel Rossetti and Oscar Wilde, and threw legendary banquets and parties for them at his home and studio in Chelsea. Whistler enjoyed entertaining everyone with his charm and wit. He dressed finely, in fitted black suits, and carried a silver-topped cane.

↑ In 1871, when his model couldn't come to the studio, Whistler painted his mother instead. She was too tired to stand up, so he painted her sitting down. *Arrangement in Grey and Black No. 1* (1871) was the result.

↑ *Symphony in White No. III* (1865-7) was the first picture Whistler gave a musical title ("symphony"). For him, the poses of the girls and their dresses in different shades of white created a balanced picture that worked like a piece of music.

Even though he was a colorful character, Whistler believed strongly that his pictures should speak for themselves. He called them symphonies, arrangements and nocturnes, which are titles usually given to pieces of music. He wanted to create a mood and an atmosphere in paint, like a composer would with musical sounds. He didn't want details about the people in his portraits or the names of the places in his landscapes to distract the viewer in any way. For example, the painting he made of his mother was called *Arrangement in Grey and Black No. 1*. For Whistler, the most important thing was the way the colors, shapes and patterns he'd painted looked on the canvas.

Not everyone agreed with Whistler's views. In 1877, his painting *Nocturne in Black and Gold – The Falling Rocket* was criticized by an important art writer, John Ruskin. In the inky-black picture of a night sky lit up with spots of flames and smoke from a fireworks display, it is hard to make out any subject at all. Ruskin, angry that such a picture should hang on the walls of an important London gallery, accused Whistler of "flinging a pot of paint in the public's face." To clear his name and defend his art, Whistler took Ruskin to court. Although Whistler won the case, he was only awarded a farthing (the smallest coin there was) by the judge. The trial cost him a lot of money, and he went bankrupt the following year. But when the picture was sold to a rich American collector many years later, Whistler was delighted.

EXTRA

THE PEACOCK ROOM

In 1876 Whistler caused a stir when he decorated a dining room belonging to a rich businessman, Frederick R. Leyland.

Leyland wanted a special room in his London home to display Whistler's painting *The Princess from the Land of Porcelain* and his collection of Chinese porcelain.

Leyland hired a designer, but when he was away, Whistler painted the walls and ceiling, and added golden decorations and peacocks. Leyland was furious, but kept the room.

In 1904 the room was bought by an American collector and shipped across the Atlantic. Newspapers reported that it was reinstalled piece by piece in his Detroit home.

MONET
FIRST IMPRESSIONS

## THE BIG IDEA	To paint pictures that capture a moment in time and the atmosphere of a scene rather than its precise detail.
## CHALLENGES Working outdoors in all weathers; people thought his art looked unfinished	**WHO** OSCAR-CLAUDE MONET **WHAT** Oil paintings **WHERE** Paris and the countryside of northern France **WHEN** From the 1860s to his death in 1926 **FAMOUS WORKS** *Impression, Sunrise*; his series of haystacks; views of the River Seine and water lilies
## BACKGROUND	As an art student in Paris in the 1860s, Monet became friends with a group of artists who wanted to do something new. For them, lifelike paintings of historical scenes seemed stuffy and old-fashioned.

TECHNIQUES
- Painted outdoors
- Loose, sketchlike brushstrokes were made quickly, to catch the light before it changed

INFLUENCES
- Japanese gardens and prints
- Landscapes by Turner and Whistler

MOVEMENT
IMPRESSIONISM
- From 1860s to 1880s
- Artists painted city life in Paris and people relaxing in the countryside
- Paint was put on in quick, bold brushstrokes

NAME: Claude Monet
BORN: 1840
DIED: aged 86
NATIONALITY: French
FAMOUS FOR: inventing Impressionism; painting the same subjects again and again; his Giverny house and garden

→ *Water Lilies* (1916) is one of hundreds of paintings Monet made of the water-lily pond in his garden at Giverny. Working from sunrise until sunset, he observed the changing patterns of light as they fell on the surface of the water.

MONET
FIRST IMPRESSIONS

Monet works in his floating studio on the River Seine ...

↑ Edouard Manet painted *Monet Painting on his Studio Boat* (1874) in the Impressionist style. He used bold, swift brushtrokes of pure color straight from the tube.

Monet said
"My garden is my most beautiful masterpiece."

↑ Monet and the Impressionists painted people in the grand boulevards, railway stations, bars and nightclubs of Paris.

It's a summer's day in 1874 in Argenteuil, just northwest of Paris on the River Seine. Claude Monet is sitting with his wife, Camille, on a wooden boat that has been specially made for him as a floating studio. He's painting the reflections on the water, thinking about the way light seems to dance on its surface. In the distance, the older artist, Edouard Manet, paints him from the riverbank.

Just five years before, Monet, Manet and other artist friends met in studios and cafes in Paris to discuss how they could change art. They wanted to paint modern subjects in a new way. Instead of working indoors for months at a time at their easels, as artists had traditionally done, they braved all weathers to paint in the open air. Monet especially enjoyed working in series, painting the same scenes again and again, carefully recording the changes in the way light fell at different times of the day, in all weathers and seasons.

↑ Monet set up a studio opposite Rouen Cathedral. Here, he painted around 30 pictures at different times of day. He completed them at his studio in Giverny in 1894. The light changes even though the building stays the same.

IMPRESSIONISM: THE FRENCH ART REVOLUTION	**1841**	**1850s**	**1862**	**1863**
Impressionism began when a group of young, talented artists decided to rebel against the established art scene in Paris. They formed a new style of painting all of their own.	Paint tubes are invented. Artists can now paint outdoors instead of in a studio.	Japanese prints are sold in Paris. Their bold colors and subjects excite young artists.	Monet studies art in Paris. Here, he meets like-minded artists - Renoir, Sisley and Bazille.	Paintings by Manet and Pissarro are rejected by the Salon, France's official art exhibition.

↑ *Impression, Sunrise* (1872-3). This picture gave Impressionism its name. It is of the port in Le Havre. The orange disc of the sun and its reflection in the water lights up the scene; fishing boats are silhouetted in the background.

↑ Monet and 29 other artists put on the first Impressionist exhibition. It took place in the studio of the photographer Nadar, on the busy Boulevard des Capucines in Paris.

But the artists' new pictures were rejected by the official exhibitions in Paris, so they put on their own show. Visitors were shocked and confused, and many critics poked fun. One called the group "Impressionists" after Monet's painting *Impression, Sunrise*. He said it looked like an "impression" or "sketch" rather than a finished picture. The name stuck.

↑ Monet created a beautiful garden at his home in Giverny, full of exotic plants and a gigantic pond. He even recreated the exact bridge that he'd seen in one of his favorite Japanese prints.

It wasn't until the 1880s that Impressionism became popular. Monet moved out of Paris to Giverny, in the countryside, and by 1890 he was rich enough to buy a large house. Here he created a garden full of colorful plants and a pond filled with water lilies inspired by the tranquil Japanese gardens he'd seen in pictures. In his huge garden studio, Monet painted these views over and over again, not stopping even when his eyesight was failing. Some people think that his blurred vision influenced the color and style of his later paintings.

↑ Monet built a large studio in his garden, and worked surrounded by his vast canvases of water lilies.

Late 1860s	1873	1874	1877	1880s	1886
Artists paint in the countryside near Paris. New railroad lines make it easy to travel out of the city.	Degas moves to Paris. He doesn't paint outdoors. He paints pictures of dancers in his studio.	The first Impressionist exhibition in Paris, where Monet shows *Impression, Sunrise*.	Cassatt joins the Impressionists. Morisot is the other female member.	Durand-Ruel organizes successful Impressionist shows in Europe and the USA.	Final Impressionist exhibition in Paris includes Seurat, Signac and Gauguin.

SEURAT
TO THE POINT

THE BIG IDEA	To make pictures that use color in new ways, influenced by the ideas of French science writers.
CHALLENGES Time-consuming technique; fellow artists doubted his method; suffered from ill health	**WHO** GEORGES-PIERRE SEURAT **WHAT** Oil paintings and soft crayon drawings **WHERE** Paris, in France **WHEN** 1880s to 1891 **FAMOUS WORKS** *Bathers at Asnières, A Sunday on La Grande Jatte - 1884, The Models, The Eiffel Tower* and *The Circus*
BACKGROUND	In the 1880s the Impressionists caused a storm in Paris. Seurat knew the group, and showed his work in their exhibitions, but he wanted to take their experiments with color even further.

TECHNIQUE
Laying tiny dots of color next to each other that blend into a different color when viewed from a distance.

INFLUENCES
- Grand history paintings, including ancient Greek friezes
- Science books about color

MOVEMENT
Post-Impressionism
- Developed between 1886 and 1905
- Artists began to use vivid colors and bold brushstrokes to express their feelings, not just to create realistic pictures

NAME: Georges Seurat
BORN: 1859
DIED: aged 31
NATIONALITY: French
FAMOUS FOR: creating grand works made of tiny colored dots; thinking about how we experience art in a scientific way.

→ Seurat made this picture of people relaxing in the countryside outside Paris from thousands of tiny dots. It's easy to see them up close, but from a distance they mix together. This is a detail from *A Sunday on La Grande Jatte - 1884* (1884-86). For the complete picture, turn over to page 49.

SEURAT
TO THE POINT

Seurat works on his grand painting, dot by millionth dot ...

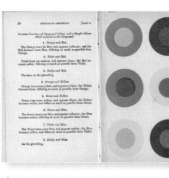

↑ Chevreul's book *The Principles of Harmony and Contrast of Colors* was published in 1839. Seurat was interested in the way he described colors affecting each other on the canvas.

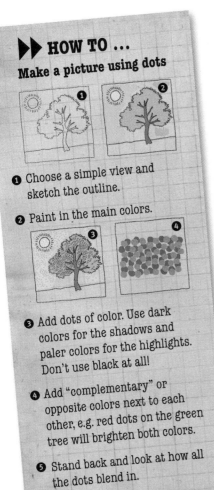

▶▶ HOW TO ...
Make a picture using dots

❶ Choose a simple view and sketch the outline.

❷ Paint in the main colors.

❸ Add dots of color. Use dark colors for the shadows and paler colors for the highlights. Don't use black at all!

❹ Add "complementary" or opposite colors next to each other, e.g. red dots on the green tree will brighten both colors.

❺ Stand back and look at how all the dots blend in.

Georges Seurat sits in his studio in Paris. It's 1886, and he's just added yet another dot to *A Sunday on La Grande Jatte – 1884*. He's been working on this painting for the last two years, and it's almost finished! In 1885, he was going to exhibit it with the Impressionist artists, but the show was canceled. He worked on it some more. Now, he's using a new technique he's invented, which will become known as "Pointillism." On the surface of his picture he paints hundreds of thousands of tiny dots in different colors. You can't see them when you stand back, as they seem to blend together, but up close they are very obvious. They seem to make the surface of his painting shimmer.

Seurat was fascinated by color, and copied out passages in textbooks by writers Charles Blanc, Michel-Eugène Chevreul and Ogden Rood. They all wrote about the way color works. By laying certain colors together, different effects can be created. Placing opposite, or "complementary," colors – like red and green, orange and blue, yellow and violet – next to each other makes both colors appear brighter. Small dots of color viewed from a distance will be blended by the eye, rather than mixed by the artist on the paint palette.

↑ *Bathers at Asnières* (1883-84) shows French workers relaxing by the Seine, on the outskirts of Paris. The city's changing landscape can be seen in the distance. There are smoking factory chimneys and a steam train crosses the bridge.

↑ *A Sunday on La Grande Jatte - 1884* (1884-86). Seurat visited the island of La Grande Jatte to look at the scenery and the way light fell on the trees and the grass. In his studio, fashionably dressed models posed for the figures.

↑ Strolling in parks and gardens on Sundays was a popular pastime for Parisians, and they dressed for the occasion. Women wore flowing skirts draped over wide bustles and elaborate bonnets.

↑ Seurat's crayon drawings helped him to work out the shapes he would use in *A Sunday on La Grande Jatte*. He probably transferred them onto the large canvas with the help of a grid.

Seurat used all these ideas in *A Sunday on La Grande Jatte – 1884*. The picture includes 48 figures dressed in fashionable clothes, three dogs and even a pet monkey, which Seurat painted right at the end. In the crowd, it's possible to spot a woman fishing, a trumpeter, a girl picking flowers and a crew rowing on the river. Seurat made around 60 studies of all the different areas of the painting. It wowed people when it was shown in 1886 at the eighth and final Impressionism exhibition in Paris.

Pleased with the effects he'd created in the picture, Seurat went back and added dots to some parts of *Bathers at Asnières*. He also returned to some of his older pictures, restretched the canvases and painted "frames" around the edges, also made of tiny dots, which he thought would help to lead people's eyes into the picture.

Seurat was friends with the artist Paul Signac, who shared his views about color. They believed this "scientific" way of working would change art. In 1890 Seurat started painting a picture of the circus, in which he wanted to show that lines pointing upward would make the viewer feel happy. Tragically, with the picture still on his easel, Seurat suddenly became ill and died at the young age of 31. Signac continued working in the Pointillist style he had developed, which had a great impact on artists right into the 20th century.

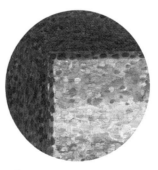

↑ Seurat didn't like the way picture frames created a shadow around the edges of a painting, so he painted his own "frames" – made of hundreds of tiny dots – onto the canvas.

VAN GOGH
STARRY NIGHTS

THE BIG IDEA	To make bold, energetic paintings in brilliant colors, which capture a mood and express feelings.
CHALLENGES Paintings didn't sell; relied on his brother Theo for money; struggled with ill health	**WHO** VINCENT WILLEM VAN GOGH **WHAT** Oil paintings; drawings in pencil, chalk and charcoal **WHERE** Paris and Arles, in France **WHEN** 1880 to 1890 **FAMOUS WORKS** *The Potato Eaters*; works made in the South of France, including *Sunflowers* and *The Starry Night*
BACKGROUND	Vincent van Gogh worked as a preacher and a schoolteacher before becoming an artist. He sold just one painting in his lifetime but produced hundreds more, many in the last two years of his life.

TECHNIQUE
Van Gogh used a special color chart to pair up "complementary," or opposite, colors.

INFLUENCES
• Japanese prints
• Landscapes by the Impressionists and Millet

NAME: Vincent van Gogh
BORN: 1853
DIED: aged 37
NATIONALITY: Dutch
FAMOUS FOR: expressive landscapes, portraits and interiors; series of sunflowers and irises; his troubled life

→ Van Gogh's colorful *Café Terrace at Night* (1888) is bursting with life. The thick strokes of color on the pavement show his experiments in laying opposite, or "complementary," colors next to one another.

VAN GOGH
STARRY NIGHTS

Van Gogh enjoys the bright colors as he paints in the Arles sunshine ...

↑ Van Gogh was thrilled by the golden color of sunflowers. He painted a whole series of them between 1888 and 1890.

↑ From Arles, van Gogh wrote hundreds of long letters to his brother, Theo. We know a great deal about van Gogh from them. He describes his paintings and his thoughts about art and books.

↑ Van Gogh cut off part of his ear after a fiery row with Gauguin. In *Self-Portrait with Bandaged Ear* (1889), made shortly afterward, he turns his head to show the bandage clearly.

Vincent van Gogh sits at his easel. He's in his studio in the Yellow House at Arles, a small town in the south of France. Golden sunlight pours in through the windows. Squeezed paint tubes cover the floor. He often works through the night by gaslight. It's September 1888, and van Gogh has only been painting for a short time. At first, he painted gloomy pictures of country life using dark colors. But now, inspired by the landscapes of the Impressionist painters he's seen in Paris, his pictures are becoming brighter and bolder.

Unfortunately van Gogh hadn't actually sold any paintings by this point. His younger brother Theo, who was an art dealer, supported him, sending money for food and rent every month. Theo also agreed to pay for his brother's new friend, the up-and-coming painter Paul Gauguin, to join van Gogh in the Yellow House. Gauguin had just returned from a trip to the Caribbean island of Martinique, and dreamed of saving enough money to go back one day. Van Gogh greatly admired Gauguin's work and was looking forward to his visit.

↑ In *The Bedroom at Arles* (1888) we can see that van Gogh lives simply and fills his house with plain furniture. His smock and straw hat hang on the pegs next to the bed, while his paintings furnish the walls.

↑ Swirls of color in a spiral pattern flow through the night sky, the village and the trees in van Gogh's *The Starry Night* (1889). He once said, "I often think that the night is more alive and more richly colored than the day."

The two artists shared a studio and together they made trips to nearby fields and orchards to paint outdoor scenes. They were careful not to spend too much money, and got by making their own canvases and cooking simple meals. But living and working together so closely proved tough for the two artists. Van Gogh's dramatic moods were difficult to live with. After only nine weeks, their arguments reached breaking point. Late one evening in December, in a rage after a disagreement, van Gogh cut off part of his own ear.

Gauguin left Arles and the two painters never met again. Afterward van Gogh was taken to a nearby hospital to receive treatment for his worsening mental health. He continued to paint from nature – the plants in the garden and the wheat fields, orchards and olive groves nearby. In 1890 he stayed with a doctor in a village near Paris, to be close to Theo.

Painting helped van Gogh to feel better again, and at this time he worked quickly. But he was still ill, and unable to recover. Tragically, he ended his own life at the age of 37. However, during his short life, he created striking pictures that became some of the best known in modern art.

EXTRA
LIFE WITH GAUGUIN

Gauguin spent a stormy nine weeks with van Gogh in Arles in 1888. In that time, they made some wonderful pictures.

They lived in the "Yellow House" on Place Lamartine. Each artist had a studio downstairs.

The artists went into the Arles countryside to sketch and paint. Both made studies of women washing clothes in the canal. Later, Gauguin made this one into a print.

Before he arrived, Gauguin sent van Gogh this self-portrait. He's posing as the outlaw Jean Valjean, the wild hero of Victor Hugo's novel *Les Misérables*.

ROUSSEAU
JUNGLE KING

THE BIG IDEA →	To paint jungle scenes, featuring wild animals and exotic plants, in a deliberately childlike or "naïve" style.
CHALLENGES No training; people laughed when his art was first shown; his pictures were difficult to sell	**WHO** HENRI JULIEN FÉLIX ROUSSEAU **WHAT** Oil paintings **WHERE** Paris, in France **WHEN** 1885 to 1910 **FAMOUS WORKS** *Tiger in a Tropical Storm (Surprised!)*, *The Sleeping Gypsy* and *The Dream*
BACKGROUND	Henri Rousseau became a painter late in life. At first, critics laughed at his "childlike" style. He struggled to sell his work, but there were some important artists who admired his paintings.

TECHNIQUE
Rousseau is thought to have used a mechanical drawing tool called a pantograph to copy pictures.

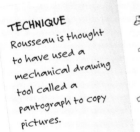

INFLUENCES
• The zoo, botanical gardens and the Natural History Museum in Paris
• Trips to museums and art galleries

MOVEMENT
Naïve Art
• A fresh approach to art, often painting popular subjects in a "childlike" way
• Artists ignored traditional painting rules or styles
• Painters were usually self-taught

NAME: Henri Rousseau
BORN: 1844
DIED: aged 66
NATIONALITY: French
FAMOUS FOR: colorful jungle pictures in which he seems to give animals human personalities

→ Rousseau's wild beast is preparing to pounce. Some people think he has been surprised by a hunter. This is a detail from *Tiger in a Tropical Storm (Surprised!)* (1891). Turn to page 5 to see the complete picture.

ROUSSEAU
JUNGLE KING

↑ In *Myself, Portrait - Landscape* (1890), Rousseau paints himself as a successful professional painter, with a beret and a smart suit.

Henri Rousseau said
"When I am in these hothouses and see the strange plants from exotic lands, it seems to me that I am entering a dream."

↑ In *The Sleeping Gypsy* (1897), Rousseau's lion creeps up to a musician dozing in the desert. Perhaps it is the gypsy's dream? The lion does not seem to be threatening her.

We're in Picasso's studio in Paris. It's 1908. Picasso has invited all his artist friends to a banquet to celebrate the painter Henri Rousseau. There's drinking, dancing and passionate speeches. In the early hours Rousseau picks up his violin and plays a waltz he has written. Everyone cheers!

People hadn't always been so enthusiastic about Rousseau. He'd shown his pictures at exhibitions in Paris for over 20 years. But his "childlike" style had been criticized and mocked, and he hadn't sold many paintings. In fact, he was quite poor and had to earn extra money by teaching the violin.

At the party, Rousseau claimed his pictures were based on the rainforests he'd seen in Mexico. But this wasn't true – he'd never been to the jungle! Rousseau sketched exotic plants, monkeys and lions in the botanical gardens of Paris. In the Natural History Museum, he drew stuffed animals from distant lands. In his studio, he copied scenes of fierce beasts and wild landscapes from illustrations in magazines.

↑ The animals in *Tropical Forest with Monkeys* (1910) stare straight at the viewer as if posing for a photograph.

↑ *The Equatorial Jungle* (1909) has a strange sense of perspective. Rousseau has painted giant flowers that tower over the monkeys hiding in the grass.

In scenes like *Tiger in a Tropical Storm (Surprised!),* Rousseau creates a lush jungle in amazing detail, from the driving rain and flashes of lightning in the sky to the trees and leaves in a kaleidoscope of greens, browns and oranges. Like *The Equatorial Jungle*, the picture has a curious sense of perspective, or space. It has no depth. It looks flat, as if it has been made from a collection of layers, like a paper collage or theater scenery. In fact, Rousseau painted section by section, finishing one before moving on to the next.

Instead of painting exactly what he saw, Rousseau enjoyed making his pictures strange and marvelous. This is why he came to be toasted by some of the leading young painters in France. They admired the unusual and exotic subjects he chose and his simple compositions, or the ways that he arranged the subjects on the canvas. His pictures suggested new possibilities for painting. These new ideas would lead Picasso and his circle to create the collages of Cubism and the dream worlds of Surrealism.

PICASSO
A NEW VISION

## THE BIG IDEA	To shake up the way things in pictures are arranged or "composed," including several points of view at once.
## CHALLENGES Initially so poor he burned drawings to keep warm; critics dismissed his paintings at first	**WHO** PABLO RUIZ Y PICASSO **WHAT** Drawings, paintings, sculptures, prints, ceramics, tapestries **WHERE** Madrid and Barcelona, in Spain; Paris and the South of France **WHEN** From the early 1900s to 1973 **FAMOUS WORKS** *Child with a Dove, Les Demoiselles d'Avignon*, Cubist still-life paintings such as *Violin and Grapes; Guernica, Weeping Woman*
## BACKGROUND	In Paris, Picasso quickly got to know the city's important artists, poets, collectors and art dealers. In 1907-8, with Georges Braque, he invented a style that would change painting forever - Cubism.

TECHNIQUES
- Picasso included newspaper clippings in his work
- He used household paint as well as traditional oil paint

INFLUENCES
- African sculptures and masks
- The geometric shapes Cézanne used in his landscapes

MOVEMENT

CUBISM
- From 1907-8 to 1918
- Many different points of view are included in one image
- Sharp, angular pictures
- Collages are made with real objects

NAME: Pablo Picasso
BORN: 1881
DIED: aged 91
NATIONALITY: Spanish
FAMOUS FOR: Cubist paintings; producing so much work; artworks fetching record amounts of money at auction

→ Picasso painted Harlequin, a clown figure dressed in a brightly patterned outfit, in his "Cubist" style. The figure in *Harlequin Musician* (1924) can be seen from different angles at the same time. Look at his face and arms, and the guitar he is playing.

PICASSO
A NEW VISION

↑ Picasso painted *The Tragedy* (1903) in his "blue" period. We don't know what the people are sad about, but the colors and their downward looks tell us they are suffering.

The story goes that Picasso's first word was "piz," short for "lápiz" – the Spanish word for pencil.

↑ Picasso's early Cubist pictures used dull colors such as browns and grays. They were rather like a puzzle - pieces of the violin and the grapes can be found in different parts of *Violin and Grapes* (1912).

↑ Picasso's *Head of a Woman* (1907) shows the influence of the African masks he saw in Paris and collected in his studio.

It's June 1907. Pablo Picasso is visiting a museum in Paris and walking through rooms full of African masks and sculptures. The galleries are damp and rotten-smelling. He wants to get out quickly. But he is amazed by the objects on display. The masks seem to be staring at him with piercing eyes. The figures are made from strong, geometric shapes. Inspired by what he's seen, he rushes back to his studio.

Picasso was taught to paint and draw by his father, who was also an artist. He showed talent from a young age. It is said that by the age of 13 Picasso was so skilled that his father handed his brushes and palette over to him, and swore that he would never paint again – though like many of Picasso's stories, this may not have been true! In 1900, Picasso started taking trips to Paris from his home in Barcelona. At the time, which we now call his "blue" period, he was painting gloomy pictures of beggars, tramps and sick people in dull colors. A great friend had just died and Picasso felt sad. Eventually he started using brighter colors and began to include figures such as clowns and Harlequins in his work. In 1904 he moved his studio to the old piano-factory buildings known as the "Bateau-Lavoir" (or "laundry boat") in Montmartre, Paris.

Picasso's great breakthrough came in 1907 when he developed a new style of painting with the artist Georges Braque. It would become known as Cubism. He painted pictures of objects – often guitars, violins or bowls of fruit – from the front, sides and back, all at once. They look as if they have been shattered into many pieces and put back together in a different order on the canvas. Picasso and Braque worked closely together and described themselves as "two rock climbers roped together." Initially their work was dismissed by a critic as "bizarre cubes." But soon they were accepted. Picasso would continue to arrange objects in a playful way in his pictures throughout his career.

When war broke out in 1914 Braque went to fight. Picasso stayed in Paris. He continued to paint, designed stage sets and costumes, and was involved with other art movements. In 1937, Picasso made his most famous picture, *Guernica*, which was a reaction to the bombing of the town of Guernica during the Spanish Civil War. He never went back to live in Spain. Instead, he moved to a castle in the South of France, set in the hills that Cézanne, one of his favorite artists, had painted. When he died there at the age of 91, Picasso was one of the most famous artists of the 20th century.

↑ Picasso was interested in all kinds of things. He even designed a stage set and costumes for the ballet *Parade* in Paris in 1917. It is illustrated here by Ethelbert White. The cardboard skyscraper costumes were tricky for the performers to dance in!

↑ When he moved to the South of France, Picasso started making ceramics as well as working on paintings and sculptures.

↑ *Guernica* (1937). Picasso wanted to show the horrors of war, so he painted innocent people fleeing from the bombs that devastated Guernica in 1937.

KANDINSKY
COLOR AND SHAPE

THE BIG IDEA		To paint bold shapes, colors and lines that do not have to look like actual objects or things.
CHALLENGES War and revolution forced him to move around the world, often leaving his paintings behind	**WHO** WASSILY WASSILYEVICH KANDINSKY **WHAT** Oil and gouache paintings, watercolors and woodcuts **WHERE** Cities in Russia, Germany and France **WHEN** Around 1896 to 1944 **FAMOUS WORKS** *The Blue Rider*; pictures with musical titles like *Improvisation* and *Composition*; a book called *On the Spiritual in Art*	
BACKGROUND	In the early 1900s, Picasso and Matisse were exploring new ways of painting in Paris. In Germany, Kandinsky created a radical style of art made simply from colors, lines and shapes.	

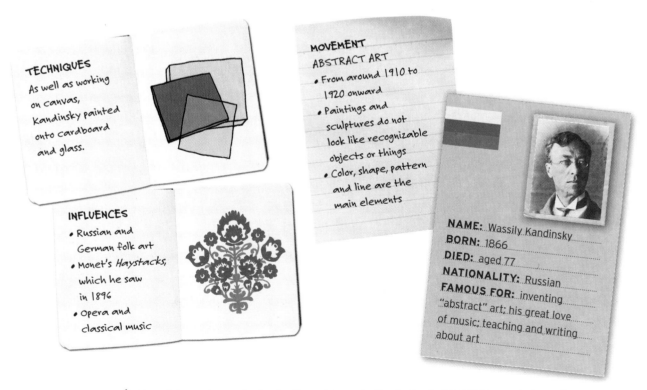

TECHNIQUES
As well as working on canvas, Kandinsky painted onto cardboard and glass.

INFLUENCES
• Russian and German folk art
• Monet's *Haystacks*, which he saw in 1896
• Opera and classical music

MOVEMENT
ABSTRACT ART
• From around 1910 to 1920 onward
• Paintings and sculptures do not look like recognizable objects or things
• Color, shape, pattern and line are the main elements

NAME: Wassily Kandinsky
BORN: 1866
DIED: aged 77
NATIONALITY: Russian
FAMOUS FOR: inventing "abstract" art; his great love of music; teaching and writing about art

→ The rainbow colors and quivering lines of *Improvisation 31 (Sea Battle)* (1913) seem to leap off the canvas and sing out, like a piece of music. As the title suggests, it's just possible to make out the sails of boats in the center. The zig-zag lines might be great splashes of water from cannon fire.

KANDINSKY
COLOR AND SHAPE

↑ Kandinsky's dancing shapes and lines in *Composition IV* (1911) were based on a castle on a hill and soldiers, but we're not supposed to recognise them.

↑ Kandinsky loved the bright colors and bold shapes of Bavarian folk art. He and his partner, Gabriele Münter, designed their home in this style and called it "The Russian House."

Kandinsky said
"Lend your ears to music, open your eyes to painting, and . . . stop thinking!"

↑ Kandinsky made a set of woodcut prints inspired by old Russian folk tales. In *Church* (1907) people dressed in traditional costumes dance in front of a church with decorated onion domes.

Wassily Kandinsky, a law professor, is at the opera in Moscow. It's 1896. Suddenly, overwhelmed by the music he's hearing, he sees a vision before his eyes – wild colors and crazy lines, sketched in front of him like a painting. He decides it is a sign – he must become an artist. In fact, we think that Kandinsky had "synesthesia," a medical condition where all the senses seem to blend together. It means that he often heard music when he saw colors and shapes, and the other way around. For him, particular colors had specific musical sounds. For example, he said that green was a tuba, violet a bassoon, and dark blue a cello.

Set on his new career, Kandinsky went to Munich to study art. He was wealthy enough to travel around Europe, and spent time in Paris and in Murnau. In 1911, one of his paintings was rejected from an exhibition, so he and another artist, Franz Marc, decided to form their own group. They called it "The Blue Rider." Kandinsky often put the image of a rider on horseback galloping through fields and forests in his paintings. Marc and Kandinsky put on their own exhibitions and created a magazine that included writing about art and music. Kandinsky also wrote poems, and a book called *On the Spiritual in Art*.

Kandinsky's pictures were bold and brightly colored. One day, he went to his studio at sunset. A painting he'd been working on was lying on its side. He liked the way he didn't recognize anything in the picture, and decided that the arrangement of the colors and shapes on the canvas was the most important part of a painting. The picture didn't need to look like anything in particular. This was the beginning of what we now call "abstract" art, which is art that does not look like an actual object or person, but is enjoyed for the way its colors, shapes and textures work together. Kandinsky continued working on abstract pictures for the rest of his career, and believed that they connected with the viewer's soul rather than their mind.

Kandinsky moved back to Russia when the First World War broke out in 1914, but returned to Germany in 1922 to work at the Bauhaus art school. Here he continued to make art, and taught classes on color and form. He was an inspiring teacher, and the passion with which he created his bright, original pictures encouraged his students to go on to make great works of their own.

↑ In *Composition 8* (1923) Kandinsky's strong geometric shapes seem to dance on the canvas. He said that different colors triggered clear musical sounds – circles were "loud" and "soft" at the same time, triangles "active" and "aggressive," and squares stood for "peace" and "calm."

EXTRA
AT THE BAUHAUS

Kandinsky taught at the Bauhaus school of art and design in Germany from 1922 to 1933.

At the Bauhaus, art, design and craft were all thought to be equally important. Furniture, ceramics and metalwork were studied alongside painting, drawing and sculpture.

One of Kandinsky's courses explored color theory. In the exercise above, a student tests the way three primary colors – red, yellow and blue – work as triangles, circles and squares.

In his first year at the Bauhaus, Kandinsky designed wall murals for an exhibition in Berlin, which his students helped him to paint.

DUCHAMP
BUT IS IT ART?

THE BIG IDEA	To bring objects from the real world into the art gallery, turning the idea of art upside down and inside out.
CHALLENGES Producing unusual and shocking art meant that it was often rejected	**WHO** MARCEL DUCHAMP **WHAT** Paintings, "readymades" and sculptures **WHERE** Paris, in France and the USA **WHEN** Around 1911 to 1968 **FAMOUS WORKS** Early paintings such as *Nude Descending a Staircase*; "readymade" sculptures such as *Fountain*; *The Large Glass*
BACKGROUND	Duchamp was part of the Dada movement. Horrified by the destruction of the First World War, Dada artists wanted to change the world they lived in. Dada art was designed to shock and break rules.

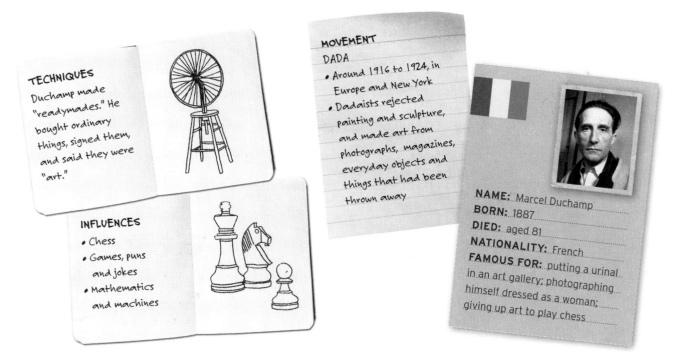

TECHNIQUES

Duchamp made "readymades." He bought ordinary things, signed them, and said they were "art."

INFLUENCES
- Chess
- Games, puns and jokes
- Mathematics and machines

MOVEMENT

DADA
- Around 1916 to 1924, in Europe and New York
- Dadaists rejected painting and sculpture, and made art from photographs, magazines, everyday objects and things that had been thrown away

NAME: Marcel Duchamp
BORN: 1887
DIED: aged 81
NATIONALITY: French
FAMOUS FOR: putting a urinal in an art gallery; photographing himself dressed as a woman; giving up art to play chess

→ Duchamp's art was designed to shock people. *Fountain* (1917) is a urinal he'd bought from a shop. It was one of the works Duchamp called "readymades" - ordinary objects that he displayed as art.

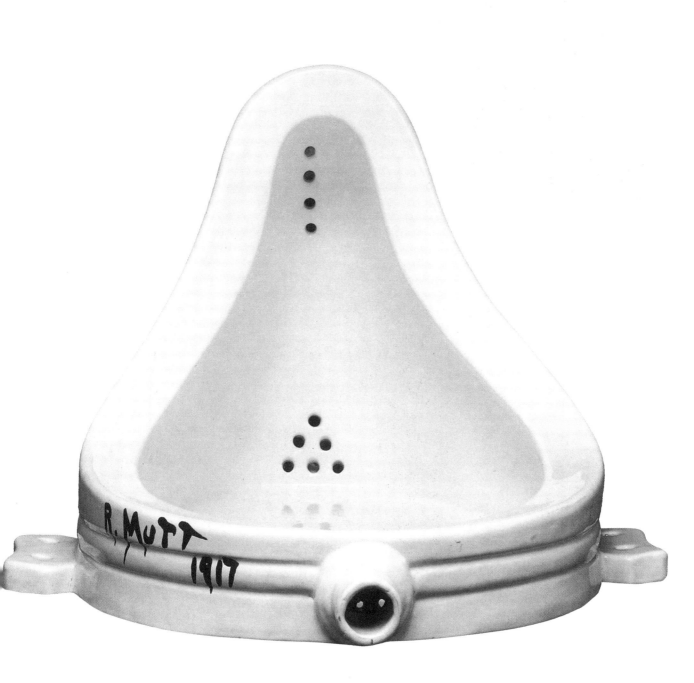

DUCHAMP
BUT IS IT ART?

↑ Duchamp loved mathematics and machinery. In 1935 he made sets of colorful spinning discs called *Rotoreliefs* that made optical illusions and patterns as they spun round on a record player.

↑ Duchamp wanted people to question the way they looked at art in galleries, so he created *Sixteen Miles of String* (1942). He covered a gallery in miles of string, and arranged for a group of children to play games amongst the paintings.

Duchamp decides to sign a urinal and enter it into an art exhibition.

Marcel Duchamp, a French artist living in New York, has a crazy idea! He decides to enter a toilet into an art exhibition. It's 1917. He visits a bathroom showroom, chooses a urinal (toilet bowl), and signs it "R. Mutt" to hide his identity. He gives it a title, *Fountain*, and enters it for the exhibition. The exhibition rule is that any artist can enter two works, as long as they can pay an entrance fee. But everyone is horrified. This is not a painting or a sculpture Duchamp has made with his own hands, but a "readymade" object he has bought. It's not surprising that it is rejected. But for Duchamp, who made the work, it didn't matter. He argued that he chose it, put it in the gallery, gave it a new title and caused people to think about it in a different way. In this way, he turned it from being an ordinary piece of furniture into a piece of art. He called this sort of work a "readymade" and said it was "anti-art."

↑ Duchamp combined an upturned wheel and a stool to make *Bicycle Wheel* (1913).

ART AFTER DUCHAMP Throughout the 20th century, artists have been inspired by Duchamp's bold works.	**1917**	**1953**	**1964**	**1966**
	Duchamp puts a urinal in an art gallery. People talk about what might and might not be art.	Rauschenberg rubs out a pencil drawing by de Kooning and displays the blank paper in a frame.	Spoerri creates *Eaten by Marcel Duchamp*, using preserved leftovers of a meal he and Duchamp shared.	Andre makes *Equivalent VIII*, a pile of ordinary building bricks stacked in a gallery.

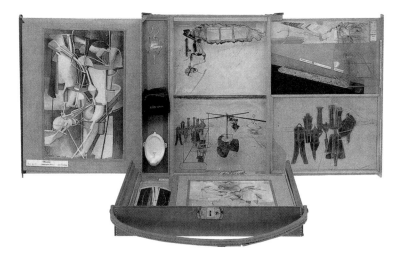

↑ Duchamp made a series of leather suitcases containing miniature versions of all his works, which could be pulled out to form a "gallery." Like his readymades, *Boîte en Valise* (1935–41) poked fun at the idea of the "unique" work of art.

↑ Duchamp was impressed by Cubism and the technique called "chronophotography," where photographers printed a sequence of shots of humans or animals in motion. *Nude Descending a Staircase No. 2* (1912) reflects this.

Duchamp had given up painting after *Nude Descending a Staircase No. 2* (1912) was rejected from a Paris gallery. No one had painted a "nude" doing something as ordinary as walking down stairs before, and he was asked to give it a different title. He refused, withdrew it, and stopped painting.

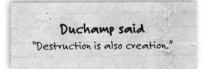

Duchamp said
"Destruction is also creation."

In 1915, Duchamp moved to New York, where he was part of the Dada movement. Dadaist work asked questions about art. Does it have to be beautiful? Do artists have to be talented in a traditional way, have special skills, or do they just need to have something interesting to say? Duchamp's work often poked fun at the art world and involved chance and jokes.

Duchamp's work had a huge influence on the art world, its critics and collectors, and on the artists that followed him. His art gave gallery visitors an important role. Instead of admiring paintings or sculptures from a distance, they had an important job to do – they now had to complete the work by deciding what it might mean.

↑ Eadweard Muybridge's photographs fascinated Duchamp. *Horse in Motion* (c. 1886) proved that galloping horses could lift all their hooves off the ground at the same time.

1966	1967	1980s	1990s	2001	2010
Nauman makes *Self Portrait as a Fountain*, a photo in which he poses as a sculpture, spitting water.	The Conceptual Art movement is born. Artists say their work is about the idea, not the object.	Koons shows mass-produced objects, such as vacuum cleaners suspended in display cases.	Levine remakes many Duchamp works in precious materials, such as *Fountain (Madonna)*.	Creed wins the Turner Prize with a work in which lights in an empty gallery space are turned on and off.	A 1960s replica of *Fountain* is installed in an actual bathroom for the Liverpool Biennial in the UK.

DALÍ
DREAM WORLDS

THE BIG IDEA	To create fantastic but realistic pictures that conjure up the strange world of dreams.
CHALLENGES Stormy relationships with his father and other Surrealist artists; very sick in his final years	**WHO** SALVADOR DOMINGO FELIPE JACINTO DALÍ I DOMÈNECH **WHAT** Paintings, sculptures, films and designs **WHERE** France, Spain and the USA **WHEN** 1929 to 1989 **FAMOUS WORKS** The film *Un Chien Andalou*; paintings including *The Persistence of Memory*; the sculpture *Lobster Telephone*
BACKGROUND	In Paris, Dalí met the Surrealists, a group of artists who made art inspired by their dreams. They wanted to discover thoughts, feelings and memories buried deep in the "unconscious" parts of their brains.

TECHNIQUES
When creating his paintings and sculptures, Dalí put surprising objects next to each other.

INFLUENCES
• Dreams and the imagination
• Rocky beaches on the Spanish coast
• Old Master painters, such as Raphael

MOVEMENT
SURREALISM
• 1920s to 1940s
• Artists and writers make paintings and poems based on the world of dreams
• They play games and develop ways to encourage their imaginations

NAME: Salvador Dalí
BORN: 1904
DIED: aged 84
NATIONALITY: Spanish
FAMOUS FOR: creating worlds from his imagination; a long twisty moustache; his business ventures

→ Tiny spheres and coiled tubes look as if they are orbiting and spinning in space! Together, they make up a picture of the Virgin Mary's face. Dalí painted *The Maximum Speed of Raphael's Madonna* (1954) at a time when he was fascinated by math and science.

DALÍ
DREAM WORLDS

Dalí paints pocket watches that look like melting cheese ...

↑ *Lobster Telephone* (1936). In this unreal, or "surreal" object, Dalí puts his sculpture of the hard shell and claws of a lobster on top of the receiver of a telephone. He made several versions of this peculiar work.

Dalí said

"At the age of six I wanted to be a cook. At seven I wanted to be Napoleon. And my ambition has been growing steadily ever since."

↑ The Dalí Theatre and Museum is in Figueres, Dalí's home town. Dalí designed it to display his paintings and sculptures. He decorated the roof of the building with a series of giant eggs, and planned its interior to be like a maze – so the visitor would feel as if they were in a strange dream.

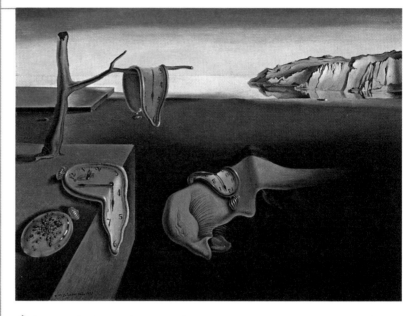

↑ To make his strange pictures, Dalí learned to enter a dream-like state. He focused his mind on particular objects, and imagined them transforming in front of his eyes. *The Persistence of Memory* (1931) includes "melting" pocket watches.

Salvador Dalí sits at his easel in Port Lligat, a fishing village on the Spanish coast. He likes to come here with his wife Gala to escape his busy life in Paris. It's 1931, late at night. Dalí has just returned from dinner with friends. He looks at his latest picture. He's painted the sea, the beach and the twisted rocks he sees in the landscape around him. Suddenly he has an idea! Remembering the melting Camembert cheese he ate earlier, he paints a group of soft pocket watches that flop over the branch of an olive tree, the side of a table and a shape that could be part of a face. In two hours, it's finished! Gala returns from the movie theatre and looks at the picture. She tells him it's "unforgettable."

Dalí called his pictures "hand-painted dream photographs." In dreams, things never stay the same for long – objects transform and change in mysterious ways, and it's hard to keep track of time. Like dreams, Dalí's pictures were often bizarre. His impossible, or "surreal," scenes were full of strange objects, but he painted them in a very realistic style using lots of detail. In these odd landscapes, we see peculiar images such as body parts propped up on sticks.

Sometimes Dalí's creatures seem to change into one another or become part of the landscape – lakes become fish and rocks become hands, arms or legs. Dalí stared at things for hours at a time until new ideas came to him. In Paris he joined a group of artists called the Surrealists, who met to play games such as Exquisite Corpse (see opposite) to inspire their work and encourage their wild imaginations.

Dalí met Picasso in Paris and was excited by his new take on art. He also dressed like his art heroes. With his famous twirling mustache he looked rather like the Spanish painter Velázquez. Dalí was famous for his wild antics and doing the unexpected. In London he even gave a lecture wearing a diving suit and helmet.

Dalí and the Surrealists didn't always agree with each other. He was thrown out of the group in 1939, and moved to the USA. Here, he worked in film with Alfred Hitchcock and Walt Disney, and made more paintings and designs. Now Dalí was an international celebrity, known for his art and his eccentric behavior. In 1948, he moved back to the Spanish coast he loved so much, and turned an old theater in his home town into a museum to display his art.

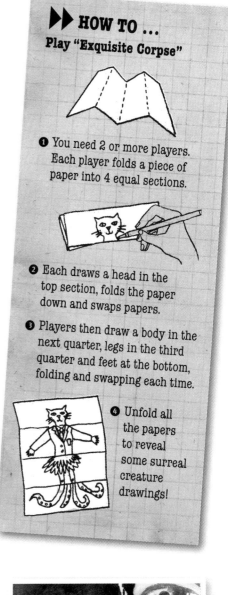

▶▶ HOW TO ...
Play "Exquisite Corpse"

❶ You need 2 or more players. Each player folds a piece of paper into 4 equal sections.

❷ Each draws a head in the top section, folds the paper down and swaps papers.

❸ Players then draw a body in the next quarter, legs in the third quarter and feet at the bottom, folding and swapping each time.

❹ Unfold all the papers to reveal some surreal creature drawings!

↑ In *Swans Reflecting Elephants* (1937), three delicate swans are reflected in a glassy lake and Dalí has made their mirror images look exactly like mighty elephants. The swans' necks become their trunks and the trees their legs.

↑ In 1938, Dalí designed a section of Alfred Hitchcock's film *Spellbound*. In it, the main character describes a dream where he is watched by giant eyes and runs through a strange landscape. It looks like a moving Dalí painting.

KAHLO
SELF-PORTRAIT

THE BIG IDEA	To paint the dramatic story of her own life onto canvas, making herself the subject of her art.
CHALLENGES Making art even when in pain; being confined to her bed, a wheelchair or the hospital	**WHO** MAGDALENA CARMEN FRIEDA KAHLO Y CALDERÓN **WHAT** Oil paintings **WHERE** Coyoacán, at the time a small village outside Mexico City **WHEN** 1925 to 1954 **FAMOUS WORKS** Over 50 self-portrait paintings, including *Self-Portrait with Thorn Necklace and Hummingbird* and *The Two Fridas*
BACKGROUND	Frida Kahlo grew up in Mexico. She began painting at the age of 18, after she was badly injured in an accident. Her pictures show her suffering, but also her great courage and determination.

TECHNIQUE
Kahlo used a specially adapted easel to paint in her sickbed.

INFLUENCES
- Mexican art
- Mexican history and traditions
- Ideas of revolution and fighting for a fairer future

NAME: Frida Kahlo
BORN: 1907
DIED: aged 47
NATIONALITY: Mexican
FAMOUS FOR: instantly recognizable, highly personal works that show her great strength of character

→ Kahlo's face doesn't show how she's feeling in *Self-Portrait with Thorn Necklace and Hummingbird* (1940), but the objects and animals do. The thorns piercing her skin reveal suffering, yet the dragonflies and butterflies indicate new life and hope.

KAHLO SELF-PORTRAIT

Frida Kahlo looks at her reflection in the mirror and begins to paint ...

↑ *The Bus* (1929) shows the scene just before Kahlo's accident. She sits on the far right, smartly dressed, with a red scarf. She's not yet wearing the traditional Mexican costumes that appear in her later pictures.

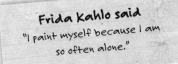

Frida Kahlo said
"I paint myself because I am so often alone."

↑ In *Self-Portrait with Monkey* (1938), Kahlo's pet monkey sits on her shoulder. With his arm around her neck, he looks as if he is protecting her from harm.

It's 1925, and 18-year-old Frida Kahlo dreams of becoming a doctor. She is heading back from school in Mexico City with her boyfriend, Alejandro. They board a brightly painted wooden bus to travel to her home in Coyoacán, a small village an hour from the city. As the driver turns into a busy junction, he doesn't notice an electric streetcar hurtling toward him. They collide, and the bus smashes into many pieces. Alejandro is not harmed, but Frida is seriously hurt. The lower half of her body is crushed in the accident.

Kahlo's injuries will affect her for the rest of her life. For three months she must lie down in bed, wearing a plaster cast that covers most of her body. She is in great pain and cannot move around. One morning, her mother brings her a special easel ordered from a local carpenter, and some oil paints and brushes belonging to her father, who is a photographer. Her parents attach a mirror underneath the roof of her four-poster bed. Kahlo looks up. She hasn't painted much before, but now she is able to paint the subject she knows best – herself!

Eventually, Kahlo learned to walk again. She decided she wanted to be a painter and visited the famous artist Diego Rivera. She asked for his opinion of her paintings – he was very impressed by her, as well as her work. Two years later, they married.

Over the next 25 years, Kahlo painted over 150 pictures. More than 50 of them are self-portraits, capturing her long, black hair and dark Mexican features. The pictures show her pain and suffering, but they also indicate that she was strong and determined. In her pictures, she includes her precious pets and possessions – the monkeys, parrots and dogs that lived with her in her Coyoacán house, the traditional Mexican costumes and hairstyles she liked to wear, the tropical plants in her garden, and other objects such as bones, insects and animals from Aztec and Mexican stories.

Kahlo had around 30 operations during her life. She was often in hospital and in pain, but didn't stop making art. She even painted onto the corset wrapped around her body. The year before she died, she had her first solo exhibition in Mexico City. Her doctors told her not to go. But Kahlo insisted. She arrived by ambulance and was wheeled in on a stretcher. Her four-poster bed followed, and much to everyone's delight, Frida Kahlo herself became part of the opening show.

↑ Kahlo taught painting classes in this room in her "Blue House." She continued working here until her death in 1954.

EXTRA

PRECIOUS POSSESSIONS

Kahlo's house was full of treasured objects, which she put in her paintings.

Kahlo was born and died in her Blue House in Coyoacán, Mexico City. It is now a museum. In 2002, cases of her special possessions were discovered in the attic and put on display.

The courtyard of Kahlo's house was filled with Mexican sculptures, tropical plants and flowers. She liked looking at them through the windows of her studio.

Fulang Chang was Kahlo's pet monkey. He appears in many of her paintings. She also kept pet parrots, hairless Mexican dogs, an eagle and even a fawn!

HEPWORTH
MODERN SHAPES

THE BIG IDEA	To make sculpture inspired by the wonders of the natural world, whether towering pieces or small, delicate forms.
CHALLENGES Forced to leave London when war broke out; it was hard to sell work and make ends meet	**WHO** BARBARA HEPWORTH **WHAT** Sculptures in wood, plaster, stone and bronze **WHERE** London and St. Ives in Cornwall, England **WHEN** Mid 1920s to 1975 **FAMOUS WORKS** *Mother and Child, Three Forms, Wave, Pelagos, Winged Figure, Single Form* and *The Family of Man*
BACKGROUND	Hepworth was part of a new wave of international artists who wanted to change the way we think about sculpture by introducing modern shapes and challenging traditional methods.

TECHNIQUES
Working without drawings or a model, Hepworth carved straight into pieces of stone or wood with her hammer and her chisel.

INFLUENCES
- Natural shapes of rocks, hills and the Cornish coastline
- Modern sculptures by Picasso, Brâncuşi and Arp

NAME: Barbara Hepworth
BORN: 1903
DIED: aged 72
NATIONALITY: British
FAMOUS FOR: works made from organic shapes, often "pierced" with holes; giant outdoor sculptures

→ Here you can see three of the nine "figures" in Hepworth's sculpture *The Family of Man* (1970). They look like giants in the landscape. Each is made with different combinations of ovals and rectangles, pierced with holes, and stacked like building blocks.

HEPWORTH
MODERN SHAPES

Hepworth carved this wooden sculpture of a sleeping baby the year her first son, Paul, was born. She called it *Infant* (1929). She has simplified the shape of the tiny body, leaving out the fingers, toes and eyes.

Hepworth said

"The sound of a mallet or hammer is music to my ears, when either is used rhythmically, and I can tell by sound alone what is going on."

Hepworth had hundreds of different tools. She used different hammers, chisels and gouges for carving directly into stone or wood, and for mixing and modeling plaster.

Hepworth looks at the shapes and the textures of the hills around her ...

The strings, tied tightly between the curves of the wood, make *Wave* (1943-44) look like a musical instrument. Hepworth said, "The strings were the tension I felt between myself and the sea, the wind or the hills."

It's around 1910. The young Barbara Hepworth is driving across Yorkshire in the car with her father. She looks out of the window at the soft shapes and textures of the hills around her. As the roads twist and turn, up slopes and down into valleys, she feels as if she is traveling through sculptures, touching their gentle forms. Later, as an artist, she describes the way this feeling of being part of the landscape has never left her. She says, "I am the landscape."

As a young artist, Hepworth went to Italy and learned to carve marble in Rome. She also visited the huge marble quarries of Carrara. Her early works, including *Infant*, were made from natural materials such as wood, stone and marble, and were based on the human figure. Gradually her work became less recognizable and more "abstract." This means that its shapes and textures could be enjoyed on their own, without them having to look like anything or anyone from the real world. She took inspiration from the piece of stone, marble or wood she was working with, looking carefully at its natural shape, grain and color, and letting this alone guide the look of her finished sculpture.

When the Second World War broke out in 1939, Hepworth, her husband Ben Nicholson and their young family moved from London to St Ives, a small village in Cornwall in the south-west corner of England. This was partly to keep safe, but also to start a new community of artists. Here she would continue to make art inspired by the landscape around her and the shapes of its rocks, hills and trees. Works such as *Wave* (1943–44) are based on natural forms – curves of waves or the circular bay of St Ives. She liked to contrast different surfaces, using smooth, polished wood on the outside of the sculpture and rough string tied tightly on the inside.

In 1949, Hepworth bought a large studio in St Ives, where she could make ambitious works in wood, stone and plaster. Her workshop spilled out onto the gardens outside, where she would carve in the open air. 15 years later she bought an even bigger building across the road – an old dance hall. Here she had room to design huge works for public spaces, such as *Single Form* (1961–64), which stands in UN Plaza in New York. She carved them in plaster, and they were then cast in bronze. Hepworth's studio and garden are now a museum, preserved exactly as they were when she died in 1975.

Single Form (1961-64) is a bronze sculpture weighing 21 tonnes. Standing outside the UN building in New York, it was made to remember Hepworth's friend, Dag Hammarskjöld, the secretary general, who died in a plane crash.

EXTRA

HEPWORTH IN ST IVES

The sunny climate of St Ives, in the south west of England, filled Hepworth with a great desire to make art.

Artists were inspired by the bright, clear light and the wild landscape of the Cornish coast. Turner and Whistler had painted here in the 19th century.

Hepworth described finding her studio in St Ives as "a sort of magic." She had separate spaces for working in different materials, and also worked outside.

Hepworth displayed her sculptures in the garden she designed outside her studio, where they sat among leafy tropical plants.

POLLOCK
DRIP PAINTING

THE BIG IDEA ⇨	To make the act of painting as important as the end result, dripping, spilling and splattering paint in a theatrical way.
CHALLENGES Needed a lot of space to make oversized paintings; struggled with the pressures of fame	**WHO** PAUL JACKSON POLLOCK **WHAT** Paintings using oils and poured household paint **WHERE** New York, in the USA **WHEN** 1940s to 1956 **FAMOUS WORKS** *Mural, Full Fathom Five, Autumn Rhythm (Number 30), Blue Poles* and *Convergence*
BACKGROUND	After the Second World War, artists flocked to New York, and it became the new center of the art world. Pollock's unique way of working and his bold paintings made him a huge celebrity.

TECHNIQUE
Pollock dipped the stick of his paintbrush in paint to drip and dribble it over the canvas.

INFLUENCES
• New York City, its bars and its jazz clubs
• Work by Picasso and the Surrealists

MOVEMENT
ABSTRACT EXPRESSIONISM
• Around 1945 to 1960
• Artists started making bold, abstract paintings that expressed their moods and feelings
• They worked on large, ambitious pictures

NAME: Jackson Pollock
BORN: 1912
DIED: aged 44
NATIONALITY: American
FAMOUS FOR: splattering and pouring paint; putting his canvases on the floor; having a wild lifestyle

→ To make *Number 8, 1950*, Pollock rolled out a piece of canvas on the floor of his studio. Paint can in one hand and paintbrush in the other, he flicked and poured layers of paint onto it, building up a thick web of swirling shapes and patterns.

POLLOCK
DRIP PAINTING

Pollock takes his canvas off the easel and lays it on the ground ...

↑ In *Mural* (1943), repeating patterns swirl and twist, tangle and turn in bold brushstrokes of black, yellow, blue, red and pink. Pollock said the work had no subject, though some of the shapes look like his earlier studies of the human figure.

Pollock said
"When I am in my painting, I am not aware of what I am doing."

↑ We know a great deal about the way Pollock made his pictures because he allowed himself to be filmed painting them. One photographer, Hans Namuth, even set up a camera underneath a sheet of glass, and captured Pollock painting on top.

In his barn studio in the countryside near New York, Jackson Pollock takes a large piece of canvas and lays it down on the floor. Brush in one hand, a tin of household paint in the other, he dances around energetically, flicking, dripping, spilling and splattering paint in all directions. He feels happy working on the floor, walking all around the picture, approaching it from all four sides. He calls this being "in" the painting.

Pollock moved to New York when he was 18, and quickly became involved in the art scene there. His breakthrough happened in 1943 when he was asked to create an enormous 20-foot-wide painting called *Mural* for the New York home of art dealer Peggy Guggenheim. The canvas was so big he had to remove a wall in his apartment so he could work on it. The picture impressed the critic Clement Greenberg, who praised Pollock and other "Abstract Expressionist" artists for their ambitious, dramatic paintings.

In 1945, Pollock married artist Lee Krasner and moved out to The Springs, near East Hampton, New York. They felt the country air would be a refreshing change from their intense city life. Krasner had her studio in the house, and Pollock starting working in a wooden barn in the garden, making giant canvases from webs of dribbled paint.

Pollock gave his large works numbers rather than titles, so that people would look at them with an open mind, without being distracted by what they were supposed to represent. Later on, he gave some of them more descriptive titles, such as *Autumn Rhythm*. Up close, the colors in Pollock's paintings marble into each other and create patterns of galaxies and constellations. He sometimes mixed sand, broken glass, coins and even cigarette ends in with the paint, and "signed" *Number 1, 1950 (Lavender Mist)* with his own handprint in the top corner of the picture. Just as important as the way the pictures looked was the way Pollock made them – one critic called them "action paintings," and compared his technique to a dance or a performance. The act of making art was now as important as the final work in the gallery.

In 1949, *Life* magazine published an article that asked, "Is Pollock the greatest living painter in the United States?" His pictures were fashionable and famous models posed in front of them in lots of magazines. But in 1951, he stopped painting in this way. Instead, he worked in black ink, and brought the human figure back into his work. Tragically, Pollock died in a car crash in 1956 at the age of 44. At that moment he was one of the most famous artists in the world.

↑ This work is called *Convergence: Number 10* (1952). The colors and patterns "converge," or join together, to create the picture. Pollock painted a background in black first and then splashed white, red, blue and yellow paint over the top.

ABSTRACT EXPRESSIONISTS

The "New York School" of artists created large, abstract paintings.

Mark Rothko used intense blocks of color in paintings such as *Untitled (Seagram Mural)* (1959). He wanted his viewers to be drawn right into his paintings and for them to react with strong feelings.

Willem de Kooning's energetic canvases layered thick brushstrokes. Works such as *Gotham News* (1955) seemed to capture the atmosphere of the bustling city of New York.

Lee Krasner's paintings, such as *Untitled* (1949), often took the form of grids filled with intriguing shapes and symbols. She called them "mysterious writings."

WARHOL
FACTORY-MADE

THE BIG IDEA	To paint pictures of America's dazzling products and famous celebrities.
CHALLENGES Very shy; shaken by a murder attempt in 1968 and never fully recovered	**WHO** ANDREW WARHOLA, JR **WHAT** Drawings, "silkscreen" paintings, prints, films **WHERE** New York, in the USA **WHEN** 1961 to 1987 **FAMOUS WORKS** *Campbell's Soup Cans, Marilyn Diptych, Electric Chair, Camouflage Self-Portrait;* the films *Empire* and *Chelsea Girls*
BACKGROUND	During the 1960s artists all over the world started making art inspired by common, everyday objects and popular celebrities. This was known as "Pop art." Warhol made art in his "Factory" studio.

TECHNIQUE
Making pictures using a silkscreen, which used a mesh screen and worked like a stencil.

INFLUENCES
• The supermarket and its brightly colored packaging
• Celebrities and comic-book heroes

MOVEMENT
POP ART
• Around 1955 to 1965
• Artists were inspired by everyday objects
• They made art that was eye-catching and immediate, in bright, bold colors

NAME: Andy Warhol
BORN: 1928
DIED: aged 58
NATIONALITY: American
FAMOUS FOR: pictures of soup cans and Marilyn Monroe; putting on a live show called *The Exploding Plastic Inevitable*

→ Warhol made pictures of everyday objects. *Campbell's Soup (Tomato)* (1962) was a picture of something that could be found on supermarket shelves. Its colorful packaging was designed to catch the eye of shoppers from rows of similar products.

WARHOL FACTORY-MADE

↑ Warhol created a huge roll of canvas with silkscreen-printed images of Elvis, which he chopped up and turned into individual pictures. With its repeating images, *Elvis I and II* (1964) looks like a strip of film.

↑ People gathered in Warhol's Factory to soak up the party atmosphere and get involved in his paintings and films. Here he also planned events and performances, and brought art and music together by managing the band The Velvet Underground.

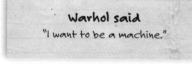

Warhol said
"I want to be a machine."

↑ Before he was famous Warhol showed his paintings in this eye-catching window display. It was designed for the Bonwit Teller department store in New York.

It's 1964. Andy Warhol is in his huge New York loft studio, which is nicknamed "The Factory." The place is buzzing. Artists, actors, musicians and dancers are gathered around, enjoying themselves. They watch Warhol and his assistants make "silkscreen" paintings of everyday products such as soda bottles and soup cans, and popular celebrities, such as Marilyn Monroe and Elvis Presley.

Warhol moved to New York in 1949 and became a successful illustrator, working in magazines and advertising. In 1961 he designed a shop display for a New York department store. He put his own paintings of comic-book characters and newspaper advertisements behind the fashionably dressed mannequins. When he heard that another artist, Roy Lichtenstein, was painting scenes from comics, he decided to paint everyday objects instead. He chose a Campbell's soup can, something he said everyone would be able to recognize.

POP AROUND THE WORLD
After the Second World War, artists made work using images from the worlds of advertising, TV and the supermarket. It became known as "Pop art."

1947	1954	1957	1961
In the UK, Paolozzi makes his first collages from magazine advertisements.	Johns paints the American flag in thick, textured paint mixed with wax and strips of newspaper.	British artist Hamilton uses the term "Pop art" in a letter to his artist friends.	In London, Blake paints himself in denim, wearing badges of his favorite bands.

Soon afterward, Warhol started making silkscreen pictures. He transferred photographs from newspapers and magazines onto canvas using a mechanical way of printing, rather like a stencil. Images could be reproduced hundreds of times, though they never looked exactly the same. His early work seemed to celebrate 1960s American culture, its promise that anyone could be a star, and the bright packaging of supermarket products. Later he introduced more disturbing images, such as pictures of car crashes and disasters.

For two decades, artists flocked to Warhol's Factory to have fun, to act in his films, and to have their pictures painted. He made hundreds of portraits of famous people. Fascinated by celebrities and their worlds, Warhol even wrote about them in his magazine, *Interview*. Making money and being good at business, he said, was "a special kind of art."

↑ Warhol made several series of "flower paintings" in different color schemes. *Flowers (pink, blue, green)* (1970) was based on a picture of hibiscus blooms he had taken from a magazine.

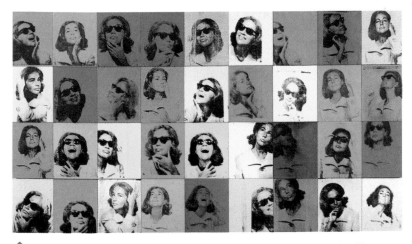

↑ Ethel Scull was an important New York art collector who was friends with Warhol. He made her silkscreen portrait, *Ethel Scull 36 Times* (1963), using a sequence of shots of her posing in a Times Square photo booth.

↑ Obsessed with documenting the world around him, Warhol gathered letters, drawings and other things posted to him in The Factory. Every day he sealed them up in cardboard boxes called "Time Capsules."

1961	1961	1962	1963	1966	1970
Oldenburg sells sculptures of food in a New York gallery, and calls the work *The Store*.	Lichtenstein makes art using pictures from American comics.	Warhol shows his "soup can" paintings. They are displayed on a "shelf" in the gallery.	Richter, Polke, Kuttner and Lueg show work in a Berlin butcher's shop and furniture store.	Richter starts making pictures based on commercial paint color charts.	In Brazil, Meireles prints political slogans on glass soda bottles.

MOVERS AND SHAKERS

Building on the achievements of the past, important artists across the world continue to make exciting and inventive work. They're constantly breaking new ground and giving us all something to think about.

ART OUTSIDE

Artists don't just make work for galleries. Nowadays, art can be found in bustling cities or out in the landscape, too.

WHO Christo (born 1935) and Jeanne-Claude (1935-2009)
Christo and Jeanne-Claude wrap up buildings like gifts! They've covered many famous buildings in fabric, including the Pont Neuf bridge in Paris (1985, above) and the German Reichstag (parliament building) in Berlin. They've even surrounded islands with fabric.

WHO Walter De Maria (1935-2013)
De Maria decided to work with nature to make his art. In 1977, he put 400 steel rods in the ground in a large desert space in New Mexico, USA. They were equally spaced to form a grid. This work is called *The Lightning Field* (1977), and when lightning strikes, the effect is dramatic!

WHO Cai Guo-Qiang (born 1957)
Spectacular outdoor "explosion events" using fireworks and gunpowder are created by Guo-Qiang. For *Sky Ladder* (2015) he made a 1,650-foot-high ladder of fireworks, which was launched into the air by hot air balloon from an island in his hometown of Quanzhou, China.

WHO Rachel Whiteread (born 1963)
Whiteread turns things inside out! For her sculpture *House* (1993), she found a terraced house in London that was about to be demolished. She filled it with concrete and then removed the outer layers of the building - its bricks, windows and roof - leaving a sculpture of the empty space inside.

MOVING PICTURES

The invention of the camera in the 1880s opened up new possibilities for artists. Modern technology inspires them as well.

WHO Bruce Nauman (born 1941)
Nauman wanted his audience not only to look at his art but to be part of it, too. For *Live/Taped Video Corridor* (1970) he used cameras to record visitors in his gallery space and projected their images back onto TV monitors.

WHO Christian Marclay (born 1955)
Marclay takes clips from existing films and pieces them together to create a completely new story. For *The Clock* (2010), he gathered enough shots of clock faces telling the time to cover every minute of the day. It took him and his assistants three years to find all the clips. The film lasts for 24 hours, and at special screenings, viewers with staying power can watch the whole thing!

WHO Pipilotti Rist (born 1962)
Rist works with video, film and moving images. Her pictures float across the walls, floor and ceiling of the gallery, while sounds fill the air. Viewers can relax on cushions to enjoy works such as *Gnade Donau Gnade (Mercy Danube Mercy)* (2013-15, below).

WHO Tacita Dean (born 1965)
The films of this British artist do not tell stories, but create atmospheric portraits, or impressions, of mysterious or unusual places. *Bubble House* (1999) focuses on a deserted house on a Caribbean island. Dean often uses traditional film cameras and lenses to make her work.

DRAMATIC ART

Artists use unusual materials and new technologies to make dramatic pieces, inviting us to look at objects in new ways.

WHO Annette Messager (born 1943)
This French artist makes sculptures and installations combining surprising objects, drawings and photographs. In *Nameless Ones* (1993), she created a room of eerie sculptures made from soft toys, stuffed birds and squirrels.

WHO Anish Kapoor (born 1954)
Kapoor made an explosive sculpture called *Shooting into the Corner* (2008–9). A cannon operated by a gallery assistant fires pellets of bright blood-red wax into a corner of the room. Over time a thick, layered painting appears on the wall, built up from layers of wax. Kapoor also makes large pieces of sculpture using fabric and stainless steel.

WHO Cornelia Parker (born 1956)
Parker asked the British Army to help her blow up an ordinary garden shed! She gathered together the blown-apart fragments and rearranged them to make *Cold, Dark Matter: An Exploded View* (1991, below). Hanging from the ceiling of the gallery, the pieces are transformed and make new shapes and shadows on the walls.

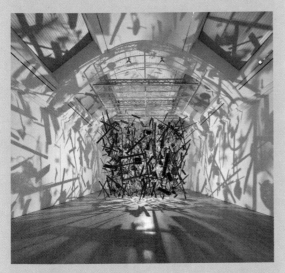

WHO Damien Hirst (born 1965)
Hirst brought dead sharks, cows and other animals into art galleries in the 1990s. They were displayed in glass tanks, preserved using a chemical called formaldehyde. More recently, he made a platinum skull called *For the Love of God* (2007), studded with over 8,000 precious diamonds.

WHO Urs Fischer (born 1973)
For his work *You* (2007) this Swiss sculptor hired a team of excavators to completely remove the gallery floor! He left a gaping 8-foot deep hole, filled with earth and rubble.

ART TO JOIN IN WITH

Since the 1960s, artists have encouraged visitors to get involved, using all of their senses as they experience the show.

WHO Yayoi Kusama (born 1929)
When you enter Kusama's rooms packed with polka-dot sculptures and mirrors, such as *Love is Calling* (2013, above), she is showing you what she actually sees. Since childhood she's experienced visions where everything is covered with dots. Art helps her to make sense of these.

WHO Hélio Oiticica (1937–80)
Brazilian artist Oiticica wanted as many people as possible to join in with his art. He made sheets of brightly painted material for them to wear as they danced to samba music. He also built *Tropicália* (1967), a large wooden labyrinth that people could enter, lined with tropical plants, sand and objects to explore and touch.

WHO Carsten Höller (born 1961)
Höller turns gallery spaces into amusement parks! Visitors can zoom from one area to another in giant metal slides and spin around above the ground in flying machines or on a carousel. He uses scientific experiments and ideas to create a thrilling, sometimes disorientating experience for his audience.

WHO Ernesto Neto (born 1964)
Cave-like spaces made from stretchy, colorful fabric welcome Neto's visitors. He wants them to relax, meet each other and discover the strange environment they find themselves in. He often stuffs spongy cushions with spices for people to touch and smell.

WHO Tino Sehgal (born 1976)
Sehgal likes to surprise! In his art, he organizes performers who blend in with the gallery visitors. In *This is So Contemporary* (2005), he arranged for the gallery security guards to jump up and sing to people, encouraging them to dance around. For *This Variation* (2012), his visitors step into an almost dark gallery with around 20 performers who sing, dance, clap, hum and talk.

GLOSSARY

Abstract art Paintings or sculptures that do not look like recognizable objects or scenes.

Abstract Expressionism An art movement that began in New York in the 1940s. Artists worked on large canvases and made bold, abstract works (see Pollock).

academy A place where art is taught. Academies opened across Europe in the 17th and 18th centuries. They organized exhibitions and had strict rules about the way art should look.

acrylic paint A quick-drying paint that is easy to mix.

aesthetic movement An art movement that started in the 19th century. Artists wanted to show beauty in everything they made (see Whistler).

Baroque A European art movement in the 17th century. Artists painted theatrical works using dramatic light (see Caravaggio).

Bauhaus An art school set up in Germany in 1919. Students learned craft and design as well as painting and sculpture (see Kandinsky).

bronze A metal (a mixture of copper and tin) that has been used to make sculpture since ancient times. It is poured into a mould, then sets hard.

brushstrokes Marks that the artist makes with a paintbrush. They can be delicate or thick, textured or smooth.

camera obscura A device invented to project images on to canvas or paper. Fitted with a lens, it worked like an early camera.

canvas A piece of rough fabric that is stretched over wood and painted on.

carving Shaping a piece of stone or wood with a chisel or a hammer to make an artwork.

cast A piece of sculpture that is made from a mould. Liquid metal is poured in, then left to set.

ceramics Art objects such as pots and vases made from clay that has been hardened in a hot oven.

chronophotography A type of photography developed in the 19th century, where lots of pictures of a

moving object are taken quickly and displayed next to each other.

Classical A painting or sculpture made in the style of the art of Ancient Greece and Rome.

collage A piece of art made by sticking different images together on a flat surface.

complementary colors Pairs of colors that sit on the opposite sides of a color wheel. Yellow and purple, orange and blue, and red and green are complementary (see van Gogh).

composition The way scenes, objects or shapes are arranged on the canvas.

critic Someone who writes and talks about art for a living, in magazines, newspapers or on TV.

Cubism An art movement that began in France around 1907–8. Objects appear to be jumbled up so that different views can be seen at the same time (see Picasso).

Dada An art movement that was designed to shock and break the rules. It was started around 1916 by artists who were horrified by the First World War and wanted to change the world that they lived in (see Duchamp).

detail A close-up view of one part of a painting or sculpture.

easel A wooden frame on which the canvas rests while the artist is painting.

fresco A wall painting that is made while the plaster is still wet. It means 'fresh' in Italian.

frieze A thin, horizontal painting, or sculpture that runs across the front of a building.

Impressionism An art movement that started in France in the 19th century. Artists often painted outside quickly to catch the light before it changed (see Monet).

installation A large work of art that fills the whole room of a gallery.

Italian Renaissance An art movement that began in Italy in the 14th century. Artists admired works by the Ancient Greeks and Romans and made paintings and sculpture in this style (see Michelangelo).

landscape A painting of an outdoor scene.

Middle Ages A period of history that began with the fall of the Roman Empire in the 5th century and ended with the Renaissance in the 14th century.

model Someone who poses for an artist.

movement A moment in art history where a group of artists share interests and ideas.

naïve art Art that looks like a child might have made it. Usually made by artists who do not have any professional training. (See Rousseau)

Northern Renaissance An art movement in the countries north of Italy in the 14th century. Artists used oil paints, and started painting subjects that were not religious. (See Bruegel)

nude A painting or sculpture of a naked human figure.

oil paint A paint made by mixing natural colors with linseed or walnut oil. It dries slowly, allowing the artist to blend the paint smoothly on the canvas.

palette A wooden board on which the artist mixes paints.

perspective A technique developed by Renaissance artists to make a flat picture look like a real, three-dimensional scene.

pigment Ground, colored materials used to make paint.

plaster A mixture of sand and water, spread on walls to make them smooth.

Pointillism A way of painting that creates pictures from millions of tiny dots of color. (See Seurat)

Pop art An art movement that began in the 1960s. Artists painted popular everyday objects in a bold, bright style. (See Warhol)

portrait A painting, drawing or photograph of a person.

Post-Impressionism An art movement that followed Impressionism. Artists focused on creating a mood using bright, bold colors, rather than painting realistic pictures (see Seurat and van Gogh).

print A picture made by applying ink to a carved wooden block, metal plate or some other surface and

pressing it on to a sheet of paper. Artists can reproduce the same image over and over again (see Hokusai).

readymade A term used by Duchamp to describe an ordinary object that is placed in a gallery and displayed as art.

Romanticism An art movement that spread throughout Europe in the 19th century. Artists made work that showed their feelings and imagination (see Friedrich).

salon France's official art exhibition. The first show, in 1667, was run by the Royal Academy of Painting and Sculpture. By the 19th century, other Salon exhibitions were taking place. 'Salon' means 'room' in French.

sculpture A three-dimensional work of art.

self-portrait A picture the artist makes of their own image.

series A group of pictures of the same subject.

silkscreen A mechanical way of printing an image on to a canvas. A fine piece of material is stretched over a wooden frame. It works like a stencil. Areas are blocked out so that paint can pass through (see Warhol).

sketchbook A drawing book for working up ideas.

studio The place where an artist works, either alone, with assistants or with other artists.

still life painting A painting of objects set up on a flat surface.

Surrealism An art movement that started in Paris in the 1920s. Artists made art inspired by dreams, often combining objects in impossible or illogical combinations. Artists played games to encourage their imagination (see Dalí).

techniques The methods artists use to make their art.

watercolor Thin paints that are mixed with water. Artists build up watercolor pictures using fine, transparent layers.

woodcut – a print made from an image carved into a piece of wood (see Hokusai).

INDEX

Dimensions are given in centimetres (inches), height before width before depth
a = above, b = below, c = center, l = left, r = right;

2 Paul Gauguin, *Self-portrait*, 1889. Oil on wood, 79.2 x 51.3 (31$^{3}/_{16}$ x 20$^{3}/_{16}$). National Gallery of Art, Washington, DC. Chester Dale Collection. 1963.10.150; **4al** Caravaggio (Merisi, Michelangelo da), *The Calling of St. Matthew*, 1599-1600. Oil on canvas, 328 x 348 (129$^{1}/_{8}$ x 137). Contarelli Chapel, S. Luigi dei Francesi, Rome; **4cl** Jan Vermeer, *The Little Street*, c.1657-58. Oil on canvas, 53.5 x 43.5 (21$^{1}/_{16}$ x 17$^{1}/_{8}$). Rijksmuseum, Amsterdam; **4bl** Claude Monet, *Water Lilies*, 1916. Oil on canvas, 200.5 x 201 (78$^{15}/_{16}$ x 79$^{1}/_{8}$). National Museum of Western Art, Tokyo. Matsukata Collection. Fine Art Images/AGE Fotostock; **4cr** Pieter Bruegel the Elder, *Children's Games*, 1560. Oil on oak panel, 118 x 161 (46$^{7}/_{16}$ x 63$^{3}/_{8}$). Kunsthistorisches Museum, Vienna; **4br** Diego Velazquez, *Las Meninas* or *The Family of Philip IV*, c.1656. Oil on canvas, 316 x 276 (124$^{7}/_{16}$ x 108$^{11}/_{16}$). Prado, Madrid; **5ar** Henri Rousseau, *Tiger in a Tropical Storm (Surprised)*, 1891. Oil on canvas, 129.8 x 61.9 (51$^{1}/_{8}$ x 24$^{3}/_{8}$). National Gallery, London; **5acr** Wassily Kandinsky, *Composition 8*, 1923. Oil on canvas, 140 x 200 (55$^{1}/_{8}$ x 78$^{3}/_{4}$). Solomon R. Guggenheim Museum, New York; **5bcr** Barbara Hepworth, Three figures from *The Family of Man. Ancestor I, Ancestor II & Parent I*, c.1970. Bronze. On Loan to the Maltings, Snape, Suffolk / Fitzwilliam Museum, University of Cambridge. Photo Sophia Gibb. © Bowness; **5br** Christo and Jeanne-Claude, *The Pont Neuf Wrapped, Paris*, 1975-85. Photographed Paris, September 1985. © Copyright Christo 1985. Photo Collection Artedia/VIEW; **6al** Lascaux Cave (UNESCO World Heritage List, 1979), Vézère Valley. Paleolithic Age, 19th-14th Millennium BC. DEA G.Dagli Orti/AGE Fotostock; **6ar** Terracotta Army of Chinese Warriors, 210-209 BCE. Terracotta figures, Xi'an, Shaanxi Province, AGE Fotostock/Mel Longhurst; **6cl** Henri Rousseau, *Tiger in a Tropical Storm (Surprised)*, 1891. Oil on canvas, 129.8 x 61.9 (51$^{1}/_{8}$ x 24$^{3}/_{8}$). National Gallery, London; **6cr** Vincent van Gogh, *Café Terrace at Night, Place du Forum, Arles*, 1888. Oil on canvas, 81 x 65.5 (31 $^{7}/_{8}$ x 25$^{13}/_{16}$). Rijksmuseum Kröller-Müller, Otterlo; **6bl** Barbara Hepworth, Three figures from *The Family of Man. Ancestor I, Ancestor II & Parent I*, c.1970. Bronze. On Loan to the Maltings, Snape, Suffolk / Fitzwilliam Museum, University of Cambridge. Photo Sophia Gibb. © Bowness; **7ar** Michelangelo Buonarroti, *Studies for The Libyan Sibyl* (ceiling, Sistine Chapel, Vatican, Rome), detail. Red chalk on buff paper, 28.9 x 21.4 (11$^{3}/_{8}$ x 8$^{3}/_{8}$). Metropolitan Museum of Art, New York. Joseph Pulitzer Bequest, inv. no. 24.197.2; **7acl** Katsushika Hokusai, *Amida Waterfall on the Kisokaido Road*, 1834-35. Color woodblock print, 37.5 x 24.8 (14$^{3}/_{4}$ x 9$^{3}/_{4}$). From *A Tour of Japanese Waterfalls*. Hotei Japanese Prints, Leiden; **7acr** Caspar David Friedrich, *Wanderer above the Sea of Fog*, 1818. Oil on canvas, 98.4 x 74.8 (38$^{3}/_{4}$ x 29$^{7}/_{16}$). Hamburger Kunsthalle, Hamburg; **7c** Wassily Kandinsky, *Improvisation 31 (Sea Battle)*, 1913. Oil on canvas, 140.7 x 119.7 (55$^{3}/_{8}$ x 47$^{1}/_{8}$). National Gallery of Art, Washington, DC. Ailsa Mellon Bruce Fund 1978.48.1; **7bc** Yayoi Kusama, *LOVE IS CALLING*, 2013. Wood, metal, glass mirrors, tile, acrylic panel, rubber, blowers, lighting element, speakers, and sound, 443 x 865 x 608 (174$^{1}/_{2}$ x 340$^{5}/_{8}$ x 239$^{3}/_{8}$). Courtesy David Zwirner, New York; Ota Fine Arts, Tokyo/ Singapore; Victoria Miro, London; KUSAMA Enterprise. Photo Scott Houston/ Alamy. Image © Yayoi Kusama; **7br** Pipilotti Rist, *Donau Gnade Donau, Mercy Danube Mercy*, from the *Mercy Work Family*, 2013-15. Audio video installation. Installation view at Kunsthalle Krems, 'Komm Schatz, wir stellen die Medien um & fangen nochmals von vorne an', Krems, 2015. Courtesy Pipilotti Rist, Hauser & Wirth and Luhring Augustine. Photo Lisa Rastl; **8al** Mural paintings decorating the northern wall of the burial chamber, tomb of Tutankhamun, Valley of the Kings, Luxor, 1347-1338 BC. S. Viannini; **8ar** Lascaux Cave (UNESCO World Heritage List, 1979), Vézère Valley. Paleolithic Age, 19th-14th Millennium BC. DEA G.Dagli Orti/AGE Fotostock; **8bl** Terracotta Army of Chinese Warriors, 210-209 BCE. Terracotta figures, Xi'an, Shaanxi Province. AGE Fotostock/Mel Longhurst; **9ar** Portrait of Paquius Proculus and his wife, from Pompei, Roman civilization, 1st century 55-79 AD. Painting on plaster, 65 x 58 (25$^{9}/_{16}$ x 22$^{13}/_{16}$). Museo Archeologico Nazionale, Naples; **9br** Discobolus Lancellotti, marble sculpture after the bronze discobolus by the Greek sculptor Myron of Eleutherae, second century AD. National Museum of Rome; **9bl** Interior of the Scrovegni Arena Chapel, Padua, looking towards *The Last Judgement*, by Giotto, c.1305, and other frescoes by Giotto lining the walls; **10cr** Giorgio Vasari, *Portrait of Michelangelo*, woodcut print. From *La Vite by* Giorgio Vasari, Florence, 1568; **11** Michelangelo Buonarroti, Vatican, showing *God Creating the World*, 1508. Frescoes executed by Michelangelo & others, 1508-12. Ceiling measures 1371 x 3901 (539$^{3}/_{4}$ x 1535$^{3}/_{8}$). Sistine Chapel, Vatican Museums and Galleries, Vatican City; **12al** Aerial view towards St. Peter's Square and Basilica, Vatican City. Imagestate Media Partners Limited - Impact Photos/Alamy; **12cl** Michelangelo Buonarroti, *The Last Judgement*, 1536-41. Fresco ceiling measures 1371 x 3901. Sistine Chapel, Vatican Museums and Galleries, Vatican City; **12bl** Michelangelo Buonarroti, *Studies of Figures and Limbs*, c.1511. Red chalk, leadpoint on paper, 17.9 x 21.1 (7$^{1}/_{16}$ x 8$^{5}/_{16}$). Teylers Museum, Haarlem; **12bc** Michelangelo Buonarroti, *Studies for The Libyan Sibyl* (ceiling, Sistine Chapel, Vatican, Rome), detail. Red chalk on buff paper, 28.9 x 21.4 (11$^{3}/_{8}$ x 8$^{3}/_{8}$). Metropolitan Museum of Art, New York; **12br** Michelangelo Buonarroti, *The Libyan Sibyl*, detail, 1511. Fresco, post restoration. Sistine Chapel, Vatican Museums and Galleries, Vatican City; **13al** General view, interior of the Sistine Chapel, showing frescoes by Michelangelo & others. 1508-12. Ceiling measures 1371 x 3901 (539$^{3}/_{4}$ x 1535$^{3}/_{8}$). Sistine Chapel, Vatican Museums and Galleries, Vatican City; **13ar** Michelangelo's design for St. Peter's Rome. From Antonio Lafreri, *Longitudinal View Showing Dome of St. Peter's, Rome*, 1513-77. Engraving on laid paper, 28.6 x 44.8 (11$^{1}/_{4}$ x 17$^{5}/_{8}$). National Gallery of Art, Washington, DC. Gift of the Estate of Leo Steinberg 2011.139.5.; **13cr** Cristoforo Munari, 1667-1720, *Still Life*. Oil painting on canvas, 67 x 53 (26$^{3}/_{8}$ x 20$^{3}/_{4}$). Pushkin Museum, Moscow. Photo Scala, Florence; **13br** Michelangelo Buonarroti, *David*, 1501-04. Marble, 517 (203.54). Galleria dell' Accademia, Florence; **14cr** Theodor Galle, *Portrait of Pieter Brueghel the Elder*, 1572. Engraving. Private collection; **15** Pieter Bruegel the Elder, *Children's Games*, detail, showing children with hoops, 1560. Oil on oak, 118 x 161 (46$^{1}/_{2}$ x 63$^{3}/_{8}$). Kunsthistorisches Museum, Vienna; **16al** Pieter Bruegel the Elder, *The Artist and the Connoisseur* (possible self-portrait), c.1565. Engraving. Graphische Sammlung Albertina, Vienna; **16cl** Theodor Galle (after Jan van der Straet), *Printers at Work*: pl. 4, c.1580/90. Engraving. National Gallery of Art, Washington, DC. Rosenwald Collection 1964.8.1578.; **16bl** Pieter van der Heyden (after Pieter Bruegel the Elder), *The Big Fish Eat the Little Fish*, published 1557. Engraving, 21.1 x 29.7 (8$^{5}/_{16}$ x 11$^{11}/_{16}$). National Gallery of Art, Washington, DC. Rosenwald Collection 1980.45.222.; **16br** Pieter Bruegel the Elder, *The Peasant Wedding*, 1568. Oil on panel, 114 x 164 (44$^{7}/_{8}$ x 64$^{9}/_{16}$). Kunsthistorisches Museum, Vienna; **17a** Pieter Bruegel the Elder, *The Hunters in the Snow*, 1565. Oil on panel, 117 x 162 (46$^{1}/_{16}$ x 63$^{3}/_{4}$). Kunsthistorisches Museum, Vienna; **17r** Pieter Bruegel the Elder, *Children's Games*, details, 1560. Oil on oak, 118 x 161 (46$^{1}/_{2}$ x 63$^{3}/_{8}$). Kunsthistorisches Museum, Vienna; **18cr** Ottavio Leoni, *Portrait of Caravaggio*, detail, c.1621. Red and black chalk heightened with white on blue paper, 23.4 x 16.3 (9$^{9}/_{16}$ x 6$^{7}/_{16}$). Biblioteca Marucelliana, Florence; **19** Caravaggio (Merisi, Michelangelo da), *The Calling of St. Matthew*, detail, 1599-1600. Oil on canvas, 328 x 348 (129$^{1}/_{8}$ x 137). Contarelli Chapel, Church of San Luigi dei Francesi, Rome; **20al** Caravaggio (Merisi, Michelangelo da), *Boy With a Basket of Fruit*, 1593-94. Oil on canvas, 67 x 53 (27$^{1}/_{2}$ x 26$^{3}/_{8}$). Borghese Gallery, Rome; **20cl** Caravaggio (Merisi, Michelangelo da), *Madonna of the Prilgrims*, detail, 1603-05. Oil on canvas, 260 x 150 (102$^{3}/_{8}$ x 59$^{1}/_{16}$). Chiesa di San Agostino, Rome; **20bl** Caravaggio (Merisi, Michelangelo da), *David With the Head of Goliath*, detail, c.1610. Oil on canvas, 125 x 101 (49$^{3}/_{16}$ x 39$^{3}/_{4}$). Galleria Borghese, Rome; **20br** Caravaggio (Merisi, Michelangelo da), *The Cardsharps*, c.1594. Oil on canvas, 91.5 x 128.2 (36 x 50$^{1}/_{2}$). Kimbell Museum of Art, Fort Worth, Texas; **21al** Caravaggio (Merisi, Michelangelo da*), The Supper at Emmaus*, 1601. Oil on canvas, 141 x 196.2 (55$^{1}/_{2}$ x 77$^{1}/_{4}$). National Gallery, London; **21ar** Pig's bladder filled with paint, black & white engraving. From P. L Bouvier, *Manuel des Jeunes Artistes et Amateurs en Peinture*, 2nd ed. Paris, 1832; **22cr** Diego Velázquez, *Self Portrait*, detail, 1640. Oil on canvas, 45 x 38 (17$^{11}/_{16}$ x 14$^{15}/_{16}$). Museo de Bellas Artes, Seville; **23** Diego Velázquez, *Infanta Margarita Teresa in Blue Dress*, c.1659. Oil on canvas, 120.5 x 94.5 (47$^{7}/_{16}$ x 37$^{3}/_{16}$). Kunsthistorisches Museum, Vienna; **24al** Diego Velázquez, *Portrait of Philip IV in Brown and Silver*, 1631-32. Oil on canvas, 195 x 110 (76$^{3}/_{4}$ x 43$^{5}/_{16}$). National Gallery, London; **24bl** Diego Velázquez, *Portrait of Pope Innocent X*, 1650. Oil on canvas, 140 x 120 (55$^{1}/_{8}$ x 47$^{1}/_{4}$). Galleria Doria-Pamphilj, Rome; **24br** Diego Velázquez, *Old Woman Cooking Eggs*, 1618. Oil on canvas, 100.5 x 119 (39$^{9}/_{16}$ x 46$^{3}/_{4}$). Scottish National Gallery, Edinburgh; **25al** Diego Velázquez, *Las Meninas* or *The Family of Philip IV*, c.1656. Oil on canvas, 318 x 276 (125$^{3}/_{16}$ x 108$^{1}/_{16}$). Prado, Madrid; **25ar** Christopher Columbus' ship *The Santa Maria*. Black & white engraving. Private collection. iStock/ Constance McGuire; **25cr** Juan de Juni, *Burial of Christ*, 1541-44. Polychrome wood sculpture. National Sculpture Museum, Valladolid, Castile and Leon. AGE Fotostock/Ivan Vdovin; **25br** Library interior, the Monastery of San Lorenzo de El Escorial Palace, Madrid, Spain. L. Deville; **26cr** Jan Vermeer, *The Procuress*, detail (believed to be a self-portrait), 1656. Oil on canvas, 143 x 130 (56$^{5}/_{16}$ x 51$^{3}/_{16}$). Gemäldegalerie Alte Meister, Staatliche Kunstsammlungen Dresden; **27** Jan Vermeer, *Girl with A Pearl Earring*, c.1665-66. Oil on canvas, 44.5 x 39 (17$^{1}/_{2}$ x 15$^{1}/_{8}$). Mauritshuis, The Hague; **28al** Jan Vermeer, *The Art of Painting*, c.1666-68. Oil on canvas, 120 x 100 (47$^{1}/_{4}$ x 39$^{3}/_{8}$). Kunsthistorisches Museum, Vienna; **28ar** Jan Vermeer, *The Milkmaid*, c.1658-60. Oil on canvas, 45.4 x 40.6 (17$^{7}/_{8}$ x 16). Rijksmuseum, Amsterdam; **28bl** Jan Vermeer, *The Guitar Player*, c.1672. Oil on canvas, 53 x 46 (20$^{3}/_{4}$ x 18$^{1}/_{2}$). Iveagh Bequest, Kenwood House, London. Historic England; **29al** Jan Vermeer, *The Little Street*, detail, c.1657-58. Oil on canvas, 53.5 x 43.5 (21$^{1}/_{16}$ x 17$^{1}/_{8}$). Rijksmuseum, Amsterdam; **29ar** Camera Obscura from Athanasius Kircher, *Ars Magna*, Amsterdam, 1671. Engraving. AGE Fotostock/ Image Asset Management; **29cr** Rough or raw example of lapis-lazuli, a semi-precious gemstone. iStock/SunChan; **29br** Black and white photograph of an x-ray showing Jan Vermeer *Woman in Blue Reading a Letter*, 1662-63. Oil on canvas, 46.5 x 39 (18$^{5}/_{16}$ x 15$^{3}/_{8}$). Rjksmuseum, Amsterdam; **30cr** Katsushika Hokusai, *Self-Portrait as an Old Man*, detail, undated. Ink drawing on paper. Musée de Louvre, Paris; **31** Katsushika Hokusai, *Amida Waterfall on the Kisokaido Road*, 1834-35. Color woodblock print, 37.5 x 24.8 (14$^{3}/_{4}$ x 9$^{3}/_{4}$). From *A Tour of Japanese Waterfalls*. Hotei Japanese Prints, Leiden; **32al** Katsushika Hokusai, *Quick Lessons in Simplified Drawing*, Volume 2, 1812-14. Monochrome woodblock print, 21 x 15 (8$^{1}/_{4}$ x 5$^{7}/_{8}$). British Museum, London; **32br** Katsushika Hokusai, *Timber Yard by the Tate River*, 1835. From *Thirty-six Views of Mount Fuji*. Color woodblock print, 25.6 x 38.1 (10$^{1}/_{16}$ x 15). Metropolitan Museum of Art, New York; **33a** Katsushika Hokusai, *The Great Wave off Kanagawa*, color woodblock print, 1826-33. From *Thirty-six Views of Mount Fuji*. Color woodblock print, 25.9 x 38 (10$^{3}/_{16}$ x 14$^{15}/_{16}$). Library of Congress, Prints and Photographs Division, Washington, DC; **33br** Color photograph of Mount Fuji. Spring-time view across tea fields. iStock/ © rssfhs; **34cr** Caspar David Friedrich, *Self-Portrait*, detail, 1800. Chalk, 42 x 27.6 (16$^{1}/_{2}$ x 10$^{3}/_{4}$). Department of Prints & Drawings, Royal Museum of Fine Arts, Copenhagen; **35** Caspar David Friedrich, *Wanderer above the Sea of Fog*, 1818. Oil on canvas, 98.4 x 74.8 (29$^{1}/_{2}$ x 37$^{3}/_{8}$). Hamburger Kunsthalle, Hamburg; **36al** Caspar David Friedrich, *The Cross in the Mountains*, 1808. Oil on canvas, 115 x 110 (45$^{1}/_{4}$ x 43$^{5}/_{16}$). Staatliche Kunstsammlungen Dresden; **36br** Caspar David Friedrich, *Abbey by the Oakwood*, c.1809. Oil on canvas, 110.4 x 171 (43$^{5}/_{8}$ x 67$^{3}/_{8}$). Nationalgalerie, Berlin; **36bl** Caspar David Friedrich, *The Chalk Cliffs on Rugen*, c.1818. Oil on canvas, 90.5 x 71 (35$^{1}/_{2}$ x 28). Oskar Reinhart Collection, Winterthur; **37al** Caspar David Friedrich, *The Sea of Ice* or *Arctic Shipwreck*, 1823-24. Oil on canvas, 96.7 x 126.9 (38$^{1}/_{16}$ x 49$^{15}/_{16}$). Hamburger Kunsthalle, Hamburg; **37ar** Open spread from *Frankenstein* by Mary Shelley, 1818. © Mary Evans Picture Library/ Alamy Stock Photo; **37cr** Stage model for the opera *Tannhauser* by Richard Wagner, (1813-83). German School, 19th century. Painted card. Private collection; **37br** J.M.W. Turner, *Snow Storm: Steam-Boat off a Harbour's Mouth making Signals in Shallow Water, and going by the Lead*, 1842. Oil on canvas, 91.5 x 122 (36 x 48). Tate, London; **38cr** James Abbott McNeill Whistler, *Three-quarter length portrait, standing, facing left*, detail, 1878. Black and white photograph. Created by the London Stereoscopic Company. Library of Congress Prints and Photographs Division, Washington, DC, LC-DIG-ds-04750; **39** James Abbott McNeill Whistler, *Nocturne in Black and Gold - The Falling Rocket*, 1875. Oil on panel, 60.3 x 46.6 (23$^{3}/_{4}$ x 18$^{3}/_{8}$). Detroit Institute of Arts, Detroit, Gift of Dexter M. Ferry Jr.; **40al** James Abbott McNeill Whistler, *Nocturne in Blue and Silver - Chelsea*, 1871. Oil on wood, 50.2 x 60.8 (19$^{3}/_{8}$ x 23$^{15}/_{16}$). Tate, London; **40cl** James

Abbott McNeill Whistler's butterfly signature, with wings raised, 1890–92. Pen and ink drawing, sheet 14.8 x 10.9 (5 13/16 x 4 5/16). Library of Congress Prints and Photographs Division Washington, DC; **40br** James Abbott McNeill Whistler, *Arrangement in Grey and Black, No.1: Portrait of the Artist's Mother*, 1871. Oil painting on canvas, 144.3 x 165.2 (56 3/4 x 65 1/16). Musée d'Orsay, Paris; **40bl** Anna Whistler, portrait of Whistler's mother, 1850s. Black and white photograph. Private collection; **41al** James Abbott McNeill Whistler, *Symphony in White No. III*, 1865–67. Oil on canvas, 52 x 76.5 (20 1/2 x 30 1/8). Barber Institute of Fine Arts, University of Birmingham; **41ar** The Peacock Room at 49 Prince's Gate, London, 1892. Black and white photograph by H. Bedford Lemere. National Monuments Record. Royal Commission on the Historical Monuments of England, London; **41cr** James Abbott McNeill Whistler, *Harmony in Blue and Gold*, details from shutter panels, the Peacock Room. Oil paint and gold leaf on canvas, leather, and wood, 421.6 x 613.4 x 1026.2 (166 x 241 1/2 x 404). Freer Gallery of Art, Smithsonian Institution, Washington, DC; **41br** Excerpt from *New York Herald* newspaper, Sunday 17th July, 1904. Freer Gallery of Art, Smithsonian Institution, Washington, DC; **42cr** Portrait of Claude Monet by Nadar (Gaspard-Félix Tournachon), detail, 1899. Black and white photograph, detail. Archives Photographiques, Paris; **43** Claude Monet, *Water Lilies*, 1916. Oil on canvas, 200.5 x 201 (78 15/16 x 79 1/8). National Museum of Western Art, Tokyo. Matsukata Collection. Fine Art Images/ AGE Fotostock; **44al** Edouard Manet, *Monet Painting on his Studio Boat*, 1874. Oil on canvas, 82.5 x 105 (32 1/2 x 41 5/16). Neue Pinakothek, Munich; **44l** Parisian ladies outside the Hotel de Ville, Paris. Sepia postcard. Undated. Bartko-Reher-OHG, Alte Antsichtskarten, Berlin; **44cl** Claude Monet, *Rouen Cathedral, West Façade, Sunlight*, 1894. Oil on canvas, 100.1 x 65.8 (39 3/8 x 25 7/8) National Gallery of Art, Washington, DC. Chester Dale Collection; **44cr** Claude Monet, *The Portal (Morning Fog), Rouen Cathedral*, 1893. Oil on canvas, 101 x 66 (39 3/4 x 26). Folkwang Museum, Essen; **44r** Claude Monet, *Rouen Cathedral, West Façade*, 1894. Oil on canvas, 100.1 x 65.9 (39 3/8 x 25 15/16). National Gallery of Art, Washington, DC. Chester Dale Collection; **45al** Claude Monet, *Impression, Sunrise*, 1872–73. Oil on canvas, 48 x 63 (18 7/8 x 24 13/16). Musée Marmottan, Paris; **45ar** The venue of the first Impressionist exhibition, 1874, the studio of photographer Nadar, in the Boulevard des Capucines, Paris. Black and white photograph by Nadar (Gaspard-Félix Tournachon). Bibliothéque Nationale, Paris; **45cr** Claude Monet, *The Japanese Footbridge*, 1899. Oil on canvas, 81.3 x 101.6 (32 x 40). National Gallery of Art, Washington, DC. Gift of Victoria Nebeker Coberly, in memory of her son John W. Mudd, and Walter H. and Leonore Annenberg 1992.9.1; **45br** Black and white photograph of Claude Monet in front of the polyptych *Three Willows* in his third studio. Private collection; **46cr** Georges Seurat, portrait of the artist, date unknown, detail. Black and white photograph, photographer unknown; **47** Georges Seurat, *A Sunday on La Grande Jatte – 1884*, detail 1884–86. Oil on canvas, 207.5 x 308 (81 3/4 x 121 1/4). The Art Institute of Chicago; **48al** A spread from *The Principles of Harmony and Contrast of Colours and their Applications to the Arts* by M.E. Chevreul, 3rd Edition, 1890; **48br** Georges Seurat, *Bathers at Asnières*, 1884. Oil on canvas, 201 x 300 (79 1/8 x 118 1/8). National Gallery, London; **49al** Georges Seurat, *A Sunday on La Grande Jatte – 1884*, 1884–86. Oil on canvas, 207.5 x 308 (81 3/4 x 121 1/4). The Art Institute of Chicago; **49ar** Parisian fashion plate, 1880s. Color print. Musée de la Mode et du Costume, Paris; **49cr** Georges Seurat, *Le Singe (monkey)*, 1884. Conté crayon, 17.7 x 23.7 (7 x 9 1/4). Metropolitan Museum of Art, New York, Bequest of Miss Adelaide Milton de Groot, 1967. 67.187.35; **49br** Georges Seurat, *Seascape* (Gravelines), 1890. Oil on panel 21.5 ÷ 30.5 (8 7/16 x 12). National Gallery of Art, Washington, DC. Collection of Mr and Mrs Paul Mellon 2012.89.8; **50cr** Vincent van Gogh, aged 19 years, detail January 1873. Sepia photograph. Van Gogh Museum, Amsterdam (Vincent van Gogh Foundation); **51** Vincent van Gogh, *Café Terrace at Night*, Place du Forum, Arles, 1888. Oil on canvas, 81 x 65.5 (31 7/8 x 25 13/16). Rijksmuseum Kröller-Müller, Otterlo; **52al** Vincent van Gogh, *Sunflowers*, 1888. Oil on canvas, 92.1 x 73 (36 1/8 x 28 3/4). National Gallery, London; **52br** Vincent van Gogh, *The Bedroom*, 1888. Oil on canvas, 72 x 90 (28 3/8 x 35 3/8). Van Gogh Museum, Amsterdam; **52bl** Vincent van Gogh, *Self-Portrait with Bandaged Ear*, 1889. Oil on canvas, 60.5 x 50 (23 13/16 x 19 11/16). Samuel Courtauld Trust, Courtauld Institute of Art Gallery, London; **52cl** Letter from Vincent van Gogh to his brother Theo van Gogh, Arles, Tuesday 1st May, 1888. The Yellow House letter sketch, paper, 21 x 27 (8 1/4 x 10 5/8). Van Gogh Museum, Amsterdam. B520 a-b V/1962; **53al** Vincent van Gogh, *The Starry Night, June 1889*, 1889. Oil on canvas, 73.7 x 92.1 (29 x 36 1/4). Museum of Modern Art, New York; **53ar** The Yellow House, no. 2, Place Lamartine, Arles. Black and white postcard photograph, 1888. Van Gogh Museum, Amsterdam; **53cr** Paul Gauguin, *The Washerwomen (Les Laveuses)*, 1889. Lithograph (zinc) in black on yellow wove paper, 21 x 26 (8 1/4 x 10 1/4). National Gallery of Art, Washington, DC. Print Purchase Fund (Rosenwald Collection) 1985.7.1; **53br** Paul Gauguin, *Self Portrait, Les Miserables*, 1888. Oil on canvas, 45 x 55 (17 11/16 x 21 5/8). Van Gogh Museum, Amsterdam; **54cr** Portrait of Henri Rousseau in his studio at rue Perrel, Paris, detail 1907. Black and white photograph by P. Dornac. Archives Larousse, Paris; **55** Henri Rousseau, *Tiger in a Tropical Storm (Surprised)*, detail, 1891. Oil on canvas, 129.8 x 161.9 (51 1/8 x 63 3/4). National Gallery, London; **56al** Henri Rousseau, *Myself, Portrait-Landscape*, 1890. Oil on canvas, 146 x 113 (57 1/2 x 44 1/2). Narodni Galerie, Prague; **56br** Henri Rousseau, *Tropical Forest with Monkeys*, 1910. Oil on canvas, 129.5 x 162.5 (51 x 64). National Gallery of Art, Washington, DC. John Hay Whitney Collection, 1982.76.7; **56bl** Henri Rousseau, *The Sleeping Gypsy*, 1897. Oil on canvas, 129.5 x 200.7 (51 x 79). Museum of Modern Art, New York. Gift of Mrs. Simon Guggenheim, 646.1939; **57al** Henri Rousseau, *The Equatorial Jungle*, 1909. Oil on canvas, 140.6 x 129.5 (55 3/8 x 51). National Gallery of Art, Washington, DC. Chester Dale Collection 1963.10.213; **57ar** Camels on public display in the Jardins des Plantes, Paris c.1900. Sepia postcard. Private collection; **57cr** Man devoured by a Lion, reproduced in *Le Petit Journal* 29 Sept. 1895, color print; **57br** Henri Jacquemart, *Lion Smelling a Cadaver*, 1855. Bronze statue, Jardin des Plantes, Paris. The Art Archive/Manuel Cohen; **58cr** Pablo Picasso painting decorations on a plate in his pottery studio at his villa on the French Riviera, 1948. Black and white photograph, detail. © Corbis/Bettmann; **59** Pablo Picasso, *Harlequin Musician*, 1924. Oil on canvas, 130 x 97.2 (51 3/16 x 38 1/4). National Gallery of Art, Washington, DC. Given in loving memory of her husband, Taft Schreiber, by Rita Schreiber. Accession No.1989.31.2. © Succession Picasso/DACS, London 2016; **60al** Pablo Picasso, *The Tragedy*, 1903. Oil on wood, 105.3 x 69 (41 7/16 x 27 3/16). National Gallery of Art, Washington, DC. Chester Dale Collection. Accession no.1963.10.196. © Succession Picasso/DACS, London 2016; **60ac** Pablo Picasso, *Head of a Woman*, 1907. Oil on canvas, 46 x 33 (18 1/8 x 13). Barnes Foundation, Philadelphia, Pennsylvania. © Succession Picasso/DACS, London 2016; **60ar** An African dance mask, mixed media. © Heinz-Dieter Falkenstein/imageBROKER/ AGE Fotostock; **60bl** Pablo Picasso, *Violin and Grapes*, 1912. Oil on canvas, 50.8 x 61 (20 x 24). Museum of Modern Art, New York. © Succession Picasso/DACS, London 2016; **61ar** Ethelbert White, *Parade*, 1920s. Souvenir print, colored by hand in watercolor and gouache on paper, 34.2 x 37.5 (13 7/16 x 14 3/4). Victoria and Albert Museum, London. Museum no. S.487-2000. Photo © Victoria and Albert Museum, London. Cyril W Beaumont Bequest. Courtesy Ethelbert White Estate. © Succession Picasso/DACS, London 2016; **61cr** Pablo Picasso painting decorations on a plate in his pottery studio at his villa on the French Riviera, 1948. Black & White photograph. © Corbis/Bettmann; **61b** Pablo Picasso, *Guernica*, 1937. Oil on canvas, 349.3 x 776 (137 1/2 x 305 1/2). Museo Nacional Centro de Arte Reina Sofia, Madrid. © Succession Picasso/DACS, London 2016; **62cr** Wassily Kandinsky, black and white passport photograph, detail, 1921; **63** Wassily Kandinsky, *Improvisation 31 (Sea Battle)*, 1913. Oil on canvas, overall: 140.7 x 119.7 (55 3/8 x 47 1/8). National Gallery of Art, Washington, DC. Ailsa Mellon Bruce Fund 1978.48.1.; **64al** Interior of Wassily Kandinsky and Gabriele Münter's home, Murnau, Bavaria. Staircase decorated by Kandinsky, 1910. Photo Simone Gänsheimer, Ernst Jank, Städtische Galerie im Lenbachhaus, Munich © Gabriele Münter-und Johannes Eichner-Stiftung, Munich; **64ar** Wassily Kandinsky, *Composition IV*, 1911. Oil on canvas, 160 x 250 (63 x 98 1/2). Kunstsammlung Nordrhein-Westfalen, Dusseldorf; **64cl** Wassily Kandinsky, *Church / L'Eglise* from *Xylographs (Xylographies)*, executed 1907. Woodcut print 13.3 x 14.7 (5 1/4 x 5 13/16). Private collection; **65ar** Exterior photograph of the Bauhaus, view of workshop block, Bauhaus, Dessau. © Dennis Gilbert/VIEW; **65cr** Heinrich Siegfried Bormann, *Four elementary colours, relations between basic forms and basic colours including green / Wassily Kandinsky's course on colour theory*, 1930. Black ink and gouache on drawing board, 48.9 x 61.5 (19 1/4 x 24 3/16). Bauhaus-Archiv Berlin. Photo Markus Hawlik; **65br** Wassily Kandinsky, Panel design for the *"Juryfreie" Exhibition, Wall B*, 1922. Gouache on black paper, 33 x 58 (13 11/16 x 23 5/8). Centre Georges Pompidou, Musée National d'art Moderne, Paris; **65bl** Wassily Kandinsky, *Composition 8*, 1923. Oil on canvas, 140 x 200 (55 1/8 x 78 3/4). Solomon R. Guggenheim Museum, New York; **66cr** Marcel Duchamp in his Paris studio, black and white photograph, detail, 1968. AKG-Images/Denise Bellon; **67** Marcel Duchamp, *Fountain*, 1917 (1964 edition). Painted ceramic, 33.5 x 48 x 61 (13 3/16 x 18 7/8 x 24). Indiana University Art Museum, Bloomington. Partial gift of Mrs. William H. Conroy, IU Art Museum 71.37.7 © Succession Marcel Duchamp/ADAGP, Paris and DACS, London 2016; **68al** Marcel Duchamp, *Rotoreliefs*, 1935. Cardboard discs printed on both sides, diameter 20 (7 7/8). Collection Alexina Duchamp, Paris. © Succession Marcel Duchamp/ADAGP, Paris and DACS, London 2016; **68br** Marcel Duchamp, *Bicycle Wheel*, 1951 (after lost original of 1913). Bicycle wheel and fork mounted on stool, height 126.5 (49 3/4), stool 50.4 (19 7/8), wheel diameter 64.8 (25 1/2). Barbican Art Gallery, London, exhibition display February 13, 2013. Photo Dan Kitwood/Getty Images. © Succession Marcel Duchamp/ADAGP, Paris and DACS, London 2016; **68cl** Marcel Duchamp, *Sixteen Miles of String*, from his installation for the *First Papers of Surrealism* Exhibition, New York, 1942. Black and white photograph. Philadelphia Museum of Art, Pennsylvania. Gift of Jacqueline, Paul and Peter Matisse in memory of their mother Alexina Duchamp. © Succession Marcel Duchamp/ADAGP, Paris and DACS, London 2016; **69al** Marcel Duchamp, *Box in a Valise (Boîte-en-Valise)*, 1941. Mixed media, 41.3 x 38.4 x 9.5 (16 1/4 x 15 1/8 x 3 11/16). Philadelphia Museum of Art, Pennsylvania. Walter and Louise Arensberg Collection. © Succession Marcel Duchamp/ADAGP, Paris and DACS, London 2016; **69ar** Marcel Duchamp, *Nude Descending a Staircase, No.2*, 1912. Oil on canvas, 147 x 89.2 (57 7/8 x 35 1/8). Philadelphia Museum of Art, Pennsylvania / Walter and Louise Arensberg Collection, 1950. © Succession Marcel Duchamp/ADAGP, Paris and DACS, London 2016; **69br** Eadweard J. Muybridge, *Animal Locomotion*: the horse in motion c.1878. Sallie Gardner, owned by Leland Stanford, running at a 1:40 gait over the Palo Alto track, 19 June 1878: 2 frames showing diagram of foot movements. Albumen print photographs. Library of Congress Prints and Photographs Division, Washington, DC; **70cr** Salvador Dalí holding his glass walking stick, Rome, 1953. Black and white photograph, detail. © Bettmann/ Corbis; **71** Salvador Dalí, *The Maximum Speed of Raphael's Madonna*, 1954. Oil on canvas, 81 x 66 (31 7/8 x 26). Museo Nacional Centro de Arte, Reina Sofia, Madrid. © Salvador Dalí, Fundació Gala-Salvador Dalí, DACS, 2016; **72al** Salvador Dalí, *Lobster Telephone*, 1938. Assemblage (painted plaster, plastic and metal), 19 x 31 x 16 (7 1/2 x 12 1/4 x 6 3/8). The Trustees of The Edward James Foundation, Chichester. © Salvador Dalí, Fundació Gala-Salvador Dalí, DACS, 2016; **72ar** Salvador Dalí, *The Persistence of Memory*, 1931. Oil on canvas, 24.1 x 33 (9 1/2 x 13). The Museum of Modern Art, New York. Given anonymously. © Salvador Dalí, Fundació Gala-Salvador Dalí, DACS, 2016; **72cl** Salvador Dalí Theatre-Museum, Figueres, Catalonia. Exterior color photograph. © José Fuste Raga/AGE Fotostock; **73br** Film still from the Salvador Dalí-designed film set for *Spellbound*, 1945, directed by Alfred Hitchcock. Selnick/United Artists/The Kobal Collection. © Salvador Dalí, Fundacío Gala-Salvador Dalí, DACS, 2016; **73bl** Salvador Dalí, *Swans Reflecting Elephants*, 1937. Oil on canvas, 51 x 77 (20 1/8 x 30 5/16). Private collection. © Salvador Dalí, Fundacío Gala-Salvador Dalí, DACS, 2016; **74cr** Black and white portrait photograph of Frida Kahlo, 1944, detail. © Corbis / Bettmann; **75** Frida Kahlo, *Self Portrait with Thorn Necklace and Hummingbird*, 1940. Oil on canvas, 62.6 x 47.9 (24 5/8 x 18 7/8). Nickolas Muray Collection, Harry Ransom Humanities Research Center, The University of Texas at Austin. © 2016. Banco de México Diego Rivera Frida Kahlo Museums Trust, Mexico, D.F./DACS; **76a** Frida Kahlo, *The Bus*, 1929. Oil on canvas, 26 x 55 (10 1/4 x 27 7/8). Museo Dolores, Olmedo Patino, Mexico City. © 2016. Banco de México Diego Rivera Frida Kahlo Museums Trust, Mexico, D.F./DACS; **76bl** Frida Kahlo, *Self-Portrait with Monkey*, 1938. Oil on masonite, 40.6 x 30.5 (16 x 12). Albright-Knox Art Gallery, Buffalo. Bequest of A. Conger Goodyear, 1966. © 2016. Banco de México Diego Rivera Frida Kahlo Museums Trust, Mexico, D.F./DACS; **77ar** Exterior photograph of courtyard at

Frida Kahlo's Blue House (Casa Azul), now the Frida Kahlo Museum, Coyoacán, Mexico City. © image BROKER/Alamy; **77cr** Color photograph of a tropical bird of paradise plant. Eva Kaufman/iStock; **77br** Frida Kahlo with her pet monkey, black and white photograph, 1944. © Bettmann/Corbis; **77bl** Interior photograph of Frida Kahlo's studio, showing her easel and wheelchair, at the Blue House, (Casa Azul), now the Frida Kahlo Museum, Coyoacán, Mexico City. © M. Sobreira/Alamy; **78cr** Barbara Hepworth in the grounds of her workplace, Trewyn Studios, St. Ives, Cornwall, black and white photograph, 1954, detail. B. Seed/Lebrecht Music & Arts/ Corbis; **79** Barbara Hepworth, Three figures from *The Family of Man*. *Ancestor I, Ancestor II & Parent I*, 1970. Bronze. On Loan to the Maltings, Snape, Suffolk / The Fitzwilliam Museum, University of Cambridge. Photo Sophia Gibb © Bowness; **80al** Barbara Hepworth, *Infant*, 1929. Burmese wood, 42.5 x 27 x 19 (16³/₄ x 10⁵/₈ x 7¹/₂). Barbara Hepworth Museum, St. Ives, Cornwall. Presented by the executors of the artist's estate 1980. © Bowness; **80ar** Barbara Hepworth, *Wave*, 1943-44. Plane wood with painted interior and strings, length 47 (18¹/₂). Scottish National Gallery of Modern Art, Edinburgh. © Bowness; **80bl** Tools used for sculpture. Color photograph. © César Lucas Abreu/AGE Fotostock; **81ar** Color photograph of St. Ives, Cornwall. © Jeremy Lightfoot/Robert Harding World Imagery/Corbis; **81cr** Barbara Hepworth, at her studio, St. Ives, Cornwall, with plaster of *Sphere with Inner Form*, 1963. Photo 2000 Topham / UPP. © Bowness; **81br** Barbara Hepworth Museum and Sculpture Garden, St. Ives, Cornwall. Photo Tony Latham/AGE Fotostock © Bowness; **81bl** Barbara Hepworth, *Single Form*, 1961-4. Bronze, 640 (252). United Nations Plaza, New York. Photo DEA/M Carrieri/AGE Fotostock. © Bowness; **82cr** Jackson Pollock, East Hampton. Black and white photograph, detail, 1956. AKG-Images/Ullstein Bild; **83** Jackson Pollock, *Number 8, 1950* (1950). Oil, enamel, and aluminium paint on canvas, mounted on fibreboard, 142.5 x 99 (56¹/₈ x 39). Collection David Geffen, Los Angeles. © The Pollock-Krasner Foundation, ARS, NY and DACS, London 2016; **84a** Jackson Pollock, *Mural*, 1943. Oil and casein on canvas, 242.9 x 603.9 (95⁵/₈ x 237³/₄). Gift of Peggy Guggenheim, 1959.6. University of Iowa Museum of Art, reproduced with permission from the University of Iowa Museum of Art; **84bl** Jackson Pollock 'action painting' Long Island. Color photograph, 1950. © Photo Researchers/Alamy; **85ar** Mark Rothko, *Untitled (Seagram Mural)*, 1959. Oil and mixed media on canvas, overall: 265.4 x 288.3 (104¹/₂ x 113¹/₂). National Gallery of Art, Washington, DC, 1985.38.5. © 1998 Kate Rothko Prizel & Christopher Rothko ARS, NY and DACS, London; **85cr** Willem de Kooning, *Gotham News*, 1955. Oil, enamel, charcoal, and newspaper transfer on canvas, 181.6 x 208.3 x 6.99 (71¹/₂ x 82 x 2³/₄). Albright-Knox Art Gallery, Buffalo. K1955:6. © 2016 The Willem de Kooning Foundation / Artists Rights Society (ARS), New York and DACS, London; **85br** Lee Krasner, *Untitled*, 1949. Oil on canvas, 61 x 121.92 (24 x 48). Collection of Mr and Mrs David Margolis. © ARS, NY and DACS, London 2016; **85bl** Jackson Pollock, *Convergence: Number 10, 1952*, 1952. Oil on canvas, 241.9 x 399.1 (95¹/₄ x 157¹/₈). Albright-Knox Art Gallery, Buffalo, NY, gift of Seymour H. Knox, Jr., 1956 © The Pollock-Krasner Foundation, ARS, NY and DACS, London 2016; **86cr** Andy Warhol, black and white portrait photograph, New York, 1985, detail. © Andrew Unangst/Alamy; **87** Andy Warhol, *Campbell's Soup (Tomato)*, detail, 1961-62. Synthetic polymer paint on canvas, 50.8 x 40.6 (20 x 16). National Gallery of Art, Washington, DC © 2016 The Andy Warhol Foundation for the Visual Arts, Inc. / Artists Rights Society (ARS), New York, and DACS, London; **88al** Andy Warhol's studio, the Factory (231 East 47th Street), New York, August 31, 1965. Black and white photograph of American fashion model and actress Edie Sedgwick (1943-1971) (center left), with others, during a party. Fred W. McDarrah/ Getty Images; **88ar** Andy Warhol, *Elvis I* and *Elvis II*, 1964. Two panels: silkscreen ink on synthetic polymer paint on canvas, silkscreen ink on aluminium paint on canvas, each panel 208.3 x 208.3 (82 x 82). Art Gallery of Ontario, Toronto. Gift from the Women's Committee Fund. © 2016 The Andy Warhol Foundation for the Visual Arts, Inc. / Artists Rights Society (ARS), New York and DACS, London; **88cl** Color photograph of the window display at Bonwit Teller department store, showing the first exhibition of Andy Warhol paintings, New York, 1961. Courtesy Rainer Crone, Berlin; **89ar** Andy Warhol, *Flowers (pink, blue, green)*, 1970. Color screen print, 91.5 x 91.5 (36 x 36). National Gallery of Art, Washington, DC. Reba and Dave Williams Collection, Gift of Reba and Dave Williams 2008.115.4946. © 2016 The Andy Warhol Foundation for the Visual Arts, Inc. / Artists Rights Society (ARS), New York and DACS, London; **89cr** Andy Warhol's time capsule collections were kept in cardboard boxes similar to this. iStock/CHAIWATPHOTOS; **89bl** Andy Warhol, *Ethel Scull Thirty-six Times*, 1963. Silkscreen ink on synthetic polymer paint on canvas, thirty-six panels, each 50.5 x 40.3 (19⁷/₈ x 15⁷/₈). Whitney Museum of American Art, New York. Gift of Ethel Redner Scull. © 2016 The Andy Warhol Foundation for the Visual Arts, Inc. / Artists Rights Society (ARS), New York and DACS, London; **92al** Christo and Jeanne-Claude, *The Pont Neuf Wrapped, Paris*, 1975-85. © Copyright Christo 1985. Photo Collection Artedia/VIEW; **92br** Pipilotti Rist, *Donau Gnade Donau, Mercy Danube Mercy*, from the *Mercy Work Family*, 2013-15. Audio video installation. Installation view at Kunsthalle Krems, 'Komm Schatz, wir stellen die Medien um & fangen nochmals von vorne an', Krems, 2015. Photo Lisa Rastl; **93cl** Cornelia Parker, *Cold Dark Matter: An Exploded View*. Installation view at The Whitworth Art Gallery, Manchester, February 2015. Courtesy the artist and Frith Street Gallery. Photo © Alan Williams/VIEW; **93ar** Yayoi Kusama, LOVE IS CALLING, 2013. Wood, metal, glass mirrors, tile, acrylic panel, rubber, blowers, lighting element, speakers, and sound, 443 x 865 x 608 (174¹/₂ x 340⁵/₈ x 239³/₈). Courtesy David Zwirner, New York; Ota Fine Arts, Tokyo / Singapore; Victoria Miro, London; KUSAMA Enterprise. Photo © Scott Houston/ Alamy. Image © Yayoi Kusama

On the cover
Front a: Michelangelo Buonarroti, *The Creation of Man*, detail, 1511. Ceiling, Sistine Chapel, Vatican Museums and Galleries, Vatican City; **Front bl:** Henri Rousseau, *Myself, Portrait-Landscape*, 1890. Oil on canvas, 146 x 113 (57¹/₂ x 44¹/₂). Narodni Galerie, Prague; **Front br:** Plate showing an oil painting easel. Engraving from Denis Diderot, Jean Baptiste Le Rond d'Alembert, *L'Encyclopedie*, 1751-57. De Agostini Editore/AGE Fotostock; **Back a:** Katsushika Hokusai, *The Great Wave off Kanagawa*, color woodblock print, 1826-33. Color woodblock print, 25.9 x 38 (10³/₁₆ x 14¹⁵/₁₆). Library of Congress, Prints and Photographs Division, Washington, DC.
Vector overlays: front & back: color paint splat. © Roman Samokhin/iStockphoto.com; **Front & spine:** color paint tube art supplies. © Aleksei Oslopov/iStockphoto.com.

For Arlo, Zubin, Quincy, and Viola

British Library Cataloguing-in-Publication Data

Designed by Karen Wilks

Edited by Sue Grabham

First published in 2016 in the United States of America by Thames & Hudson Inc., 500 Fifth Avenue, New York, New York 10110

thamesandhudsonusa.com

Library of Congress Catalogue Number 2015943663

ISBN 978-0-500-65065-3

Printed and bound in China by Everbest Printing Co. Ltd